· LEARN ·
JAPANESE
for Beginners

LEARN JAPANESE
Hiragana
& Katakana

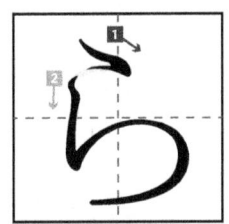 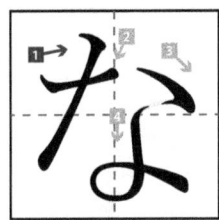 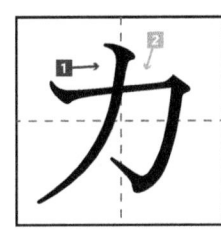 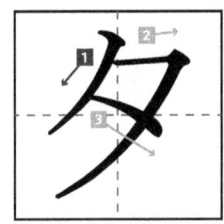

NEW 2-IN-1 DOUBLE WORKBOOK EDITION

© Copyright 2020 George Tanaka
All Rights Reserved

POLYSCHOLAR

www.polyscholar.com

Legal Notice: This book is copyright protected. This book is only for personal use. The content contained within this book may not be reproduced, duplicated or transmitted without direct written permission from the author or the publisher. You cannot amend, distribute, sell, use, quote or paraphrase any part of the content within this book, without the consent of the author or publisher.

© Copyright 2020 George Tanaka
All Rights Reserved

POLYSCHOLAR

www.polyscholar.com

Legal Notice: This book is copyright protected. This book is only for personal use. The content contained within this book may not be reproduced, duplicated or transmitted without direct written permission from the author or the publisher. You cannot amend, distribute, sell, use, quote or paraphrase any part of the content within this book, without the consent of the author or publisher.

CONTENTS

PART 1 Introduction 4
How to Use This Book 4
Background Information 5
Writing Tips 7

PART 2 Hiragana Charts & Basic Rules 9

PART 3 Learn to Write Hiragana 14

PART 4 Katakana Charts & Basic Rules 61

PART 5 Learn to Write Katakana 66

PART 6 Genkouyoushi 113

PART 7 Flash Cards 146

Tip: *This book works best with gel pens, pencils, biros and similar media. Take care with markers and ink, as heavy or wet media may result in paper bleed or transfer through to the pages below. Here are some test boxes to check how suitable your pens will be:*

Introduction

LEARNING JAPANESE

The first steps in learning to read, write and speak Japanese are learning **Hiragana** & **Katakana!** If you start by looking up charts of the characters, it soon becomes a daunting task - but this book has been designed to make it **easier** and **quicker** to get to grips with.

We will start by going over some basic background information to give you a better understanding of how the whole language system works. Then, after our *brief* look at the different 'alphabets' *(yes, there is more than one!)* we'll jump straight into learning the Kana!

HOW TO USE THIS BOOK

As with learning any language, repetition is one of the fastest ways to soak it up. This workbook contains carefully-designed instruction pages that will teach you how to write each character, with space to practice your new-found Japanese calligraphy knowledge:

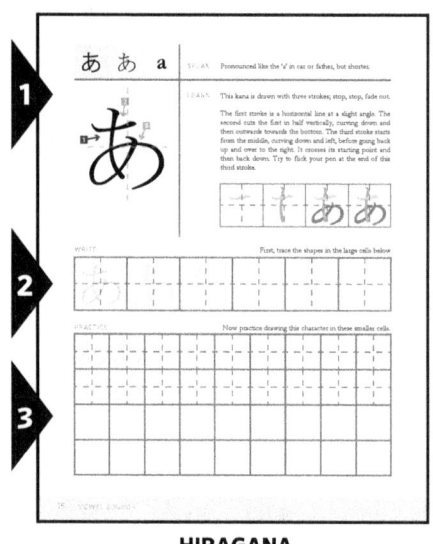
HIRAGANA

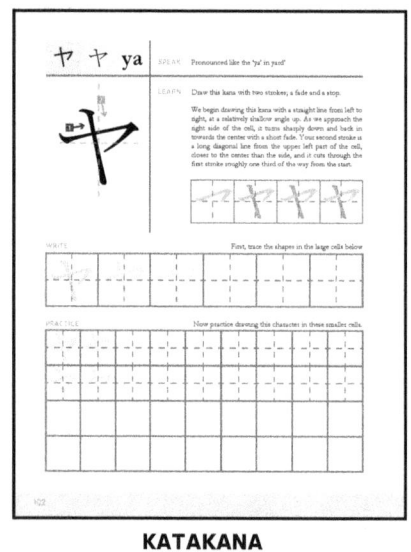
KATAKANA

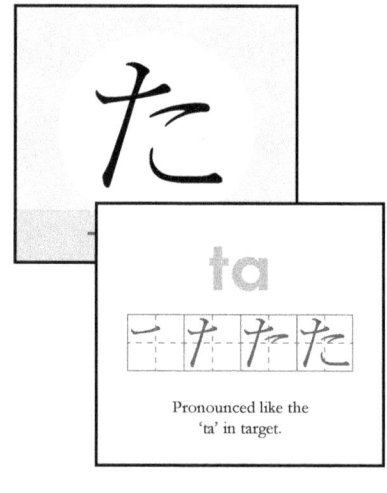
FLASH CARDS

Towards the back of this workbook you will find additional grids that you can use after you learn how to write some *(or even all)* of the Kana - these grid pages are referred to traditionally as *Genkouyoushi (or* 原稿用紙 *in Japanese)* which means 'manuscript paper'.

The final part of this workbook contains a set of flash card style pages that can either be photocopied or cut out. They are a great way to help you memorize the symbols and test your knowledge. *Younger learners should seek help from an adult to cut them out!*

Background

JAPANESE SCRIPTS

As you learn Japanese, you will encounter four very different types of scripts *(or alphabets)*. While this might sound complicated at first, it should start to make much more sense in a moment - especially as you will already understand one of them!

RŌMAJI ロマンジ

Literally meaning 'roman letters', this is really just a representation of the Japanese language using familiar English letters. It is only used to translate the language into a form that non-Japanese speakers can understand. It is not that common in every day use.

The other three scripts, **Hiragana**, **Katakana**, and **Kanji**, are used all the time and they are typically combined to make words and sentences in everyday Japanese writing. Each script has it's own purpose and together they tell us what words mean, where they come from, and also how they should be said.

HIRAGANA ひらがな

あいうえおかきくけこ

This is the first script we should learn and it consists of simple characters made with *round* shapes. Unlike the English alphabet, it is a **phonetic script** and each character represents a syllable sound. Each time you see a specific character, you will know how it sounds.

KATAKANA カタカナ

アイウエオカキクケコ

This is also a simple phonetic script. Katakana **represent the same syllable sounds as Hiragana** but are used for words *loaned* from other languages, such as foreign names, modern technologies, or foods, for example. Their appearance is more *angular and spikey*.

Background

KANJI 漢字

Translated as 'Chinese letters', **Kanji** are characters borrowed from the Chinese language. Unlike the other scripts that represent sounds, **Kanji** symbols show blocks of meaning, like whole words, or a general idea about something.

年本月生米前合事社京

There are literally *thousands* of Kanji, and new ones are being created all the time, so they are quite a challenge for even the most advanced linguists. There is some logic to how they are made so *eventually* you can understand or guess symbols you haven't seen before.

KANA SYLLABARIES

Hiragana and Katakana (broadly known as Kana) each have **46 basic** characters that, unlike English letters, represent a different spoken sound *(instead of a letter)*. Virtually all of these sounds are based on just 5 'vowels sounds' that we add a consonant sound in front of to make new ones. *I promise it will be easier than it seems!*

Hiragana	あ	い	う	え	お
Katakana	ア	イ	ウ	エ	オ
Romaji	a	i	u	e	o
Pronunciation	'ah'	'ee'	'oo'	'eh'	'oh'

The Five Vowel Sounds

This book will show you how to write all the basic Hiragana and Katakana, and also how extra sounds are created by combining the basic symbols. By the end of the book, you will be able to write the characters that make up most of the sounds needed for Japanese.

The next few pages contain a lot of information but try not to let this overwhelm you. In addition to charts of all the basic Kana that you will learn, we will break down some of the basic rules to combining these symbols - then it's time to put pen to paper!

Writing Tips

WRITING DIRECTION

Japanese texts are often seen arranged in vertical columns that are written and read from top to bottom one column at a time, starting at the right side of the page. Since the end of the Second World War, the more familiar horizontal orientation is used - read from left to right just as in the English language. This applies to all of the different scripts.

The text in these examples is identical, except for the reading and writing direction:

私は犬を飼っています。
彼女は行儀が良い。
彼らは寝るのが好きです。
多くの場合、一日中。
多分彼女は怠け者です。

Tategaki
縦書き
('vertical writing')

私は犬を飼っています。
彼女は行儀が良い。
彼らは寝るのが好きです。
多くの場合、一日中。
多分彼女は怠け者です。

Yokogaki
横書き
('horizontal writing')

Both of these styles are accepted and are often chosen based on the layout and design of the document. Generally speaking, vertical layouts are used for traditional texts, while horizontal text is found in more modern writing or on official documents. One thing to remember is that books with the *tategaki* (vertical) writing style are bound the opposite way to English books, so you actually start reading them from the back cover!

PRONUNCIATION

Learning to pronounce Japanese well starts when you learn the Kana scripts, as they cover most of the sounds we need for the whole language. It's important to practice at this early stage if you want to develop a natural and native sounding accent.

Note: This workbook includes a very basic introduction to Japanese pronunciation, as this is taught most effectively with audio. Each of the practice pages uses a similar sounding word or syllable from English to describe the sounds - it is good practice to repeat them out loud as you progress through the book.

Writing Tips

STROKES & LINES

Japanese scripts were originally written with a brush and have an inky, painted look. We use modern pens nowadays but it's important that we learn to write with the traditional movements and **strokes**. Conveniently, the Hiragana character け *(or 'ke')* contains each of the three types of stroke you will use - to help describe how to write the characters in the next chapter, we have given them names that reflect how they are made and look:

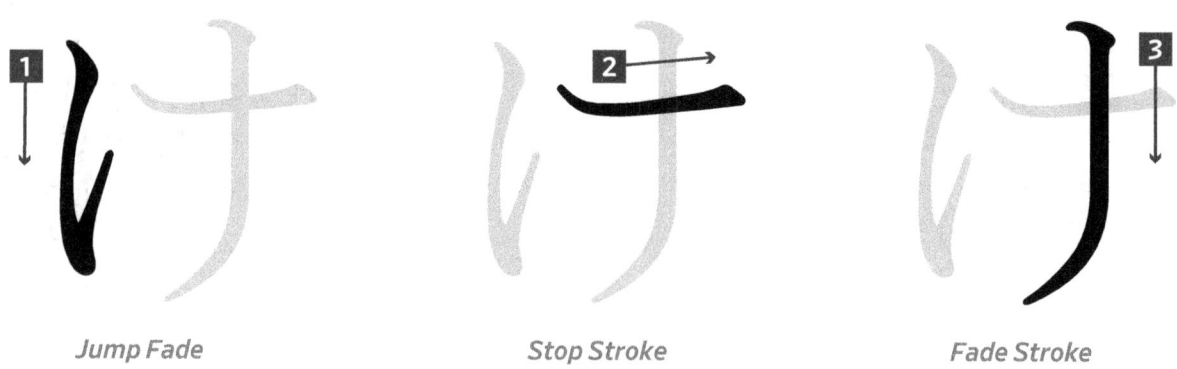

Jump Fade   *Stop Stroke*   *Fade Stroke*

The **'jump fade'** is made with a quick flick of the pen from the paper at the end of that stroke. The **'stop stroke'** is exactly what it sounds like, where your line is brought to a definite stop before lifting your pen. A **'fade stroke'** is made by lifting your pen more gently from the paper while your hand is in motion. You can imagine how the line might get thinner and fade out if you were gradually lifting a thick, wet brush tip from the page.

WRITING STYLES

This book will teach you how to write Hiragana with the standard movements based on brushed appearances, but you will encounter other styles of characters as you learn:

These characters all have the same meaning but just look a little different because they are made either by hand, with pens or pencils, or displayed as a modern digital font on a screen (or in print). Even though the appearance changes slightly, the meaning remains.

Part 2
HIRAGANA CHARTS & BASIC RULES

Hiragana Chart

This chart shows the 46 basic Hiragana with a *spelling* in Romaji for a similar phonetic sound. The vowel sounds are at the top and their counterpart versions with consonant sounds are shown below them. **note the exception 'n' - also, *wo is an uncommon kana.*

Vowel Sounds

	a	i	u	e	o
	あ a	い i	う u	え e	お o
k	か ka	き ki	く ku	け ke	こ ko
s	さ sa	し shi	す su	せ se	そ so
t	た ta	ち chi	つ tsu	て te	と to
n	な na	に ni	ぬ nu	ね ne	の no
h	は ha	ひ hi	ふ fu	へ he	ほ ho
m	ま ma	み mi	む mu	め me	も mo
y	や ya		ゆ yu		よ yo
r	ら ra	り ri	る ru	れ re	ろ ro
w	わ wa		ん **n		を *wo

Consonants

Modifiers

DIACRITICS

In addition to the *basic Hiragana*, there are **25 Diacritic** symbols. These are for similar sounding syllables that are voiced differently. They are essentially the same basic symbols but with extra marks to show they should be pronounced with a slightly altered sound:

	Basic	with Dakuten	with Handakuten
	は ha	ば ba	ぱ pa

Basic Hiragana with these small strokes *(Dakuten)* or a circle *(Handakuten)* above them show that the consonant part of the sound needs to be changed when spoken:

- **k**-sound are pronounced with a **g**-sound.
- **s**-sounds change to a **z**-sound *(except for し)*.
- **t**-sounds become **d**-sounds.
- **h**-sounds become **b**-sounds with *Dakuten*.
  ...or **P**-sounds with the *Handakuten*.

	a	i	u	e	o
k ▶ g	が ga	ぎ gi	ぐ gu	げ ge	ご go
s ▶ z	ざ za	じ ji	ず zu	ぜ ze	ぞ zo
t ▶ d	だ da	ぢ dzi (ji)	づ dzu	で de	ど do
h ▶ b	ば ba	び bi	ぶ bu	べ be	ぼ bo
h ▶ p	ぱ pa	ぴ pi	ぷ pu	ぺ pe	ぽ po

Modifiers 11

DIGRAPHS

This set of symbols are called **Digraphs** - using two basic characters we have already seen, they show where two syllable sounds are combined to create a new one:

き + や = きゃ
(ki)   (ya)   (kya)

When writing these letters, it is vital that the second symbol is drawn noticeably smaller than the first. This is how we can tell that the two sounds should be combined.

Pronunciation of these so-called *compound Hiragana* sounds is quite simple - for example, き (ki) + や (ya) becomes きゃ (kya) and we pronounce it like 'kiya' *without the 'i' sound*.

Don't let the chart below scare you - all of the Digraphs are made *exclusively* with letters from the い/i column *(excluding itself)* **and** they are only modified by letters from row **Y**!

きゃ	きゅ	きょ	ぎゃ	ぎゅ	ぎょ
kya	kyu	kyo	gya	gyu	gyo
しゃ	しゅ	しょ	じゃ	じゅ	じょ
sha	shu	sho	ja	ju	jo
ちゃ	ちゅ	ちょ	にゃ	にゅ	にょ
cha	chu	cho	nya	nyu	nyo
ひゃ	ひゅ	ひょ	びゃ	びゅ	びょ
hya	hyu	hyo	bya	byu	byo
ぴゃ	ぴゅ	ぴょ	りゃ	りゅ	りょ
pya	pyu	pyo	rya	ryu	ryo
みゃ	みゅ	みょ			
mya	myu	myo			

Modifiers

Modifiers

DOUBLE CONSONANTS

We also need to be aware that some Japanese words contain a *double consonant sound*. When writing these words, we add an extra symbol in the form of a small つ/**tsu** *(called sokuon)* to show that it needs to be pronounced differently. Let's look at an example:

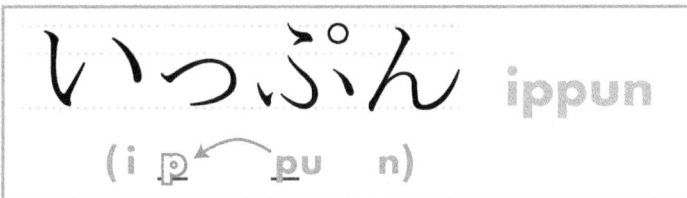

Without the small つ *(tsu)*, the word いぷん *(ipun)* doesn't have any meaning but いっぷん *(ippun)*, with the *sokuon*, means (a) minute.

Notice that the small つ is placed **before** the character that it takes the extra consonant sound from. When you see words with this modifier, the consonant part of the symbol that follows it *(in this example, the 'p' from 'pu')* is added to the end of the sound before it.

Both consonants need to be heard separately when the word is spoken, like saying **'ip-pun'** but without leaving a gap than can be heard.

LONG VOWEL SOUNDS

Just as there are double consonant sounds, we need to be aware of elongated vowel sounds too *(e.g. aa, ii. oo, ee, and uu)*. When speaking, we simply extend the duration of the sound (usually double) but in writing these words, the long vowel sound is shown with an additional character *(called a chouon)*. The character used varies depending on the vowel:

Vowel	Extender
a	あ
i / e	い
u / o	う

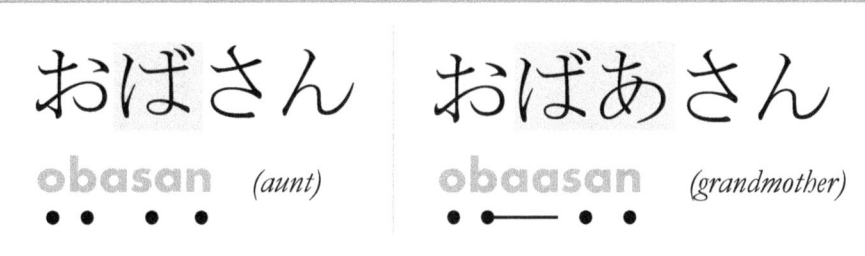

Here is an example to show how the meaning of the word is changed by adding (or missing) the longer vowel sound!

The Japanese language is full of exceptions but they tend to be learned with experience. It's just useful to be aware of double consonants and vowels for now, so you can understand when you see one!

Part 3

LEARN HOW TO WRITE HIRAGANA

あ　あ　a

SPEAK — Pronounced like the 'a' in car or father, but shorter.

LEARN — This kana is drawn with three strokes; stop, stop, fade out.

The first stroke is a horizontal line at a slight angle. The second cuts the first in half vertically, curving down and then outwards towards the bottom. The third stroke starts from the middle, curving down and left, before going back up and over to the right. It crosses its starting point and then back down. Try to flick your pen at the end of this third stroke.

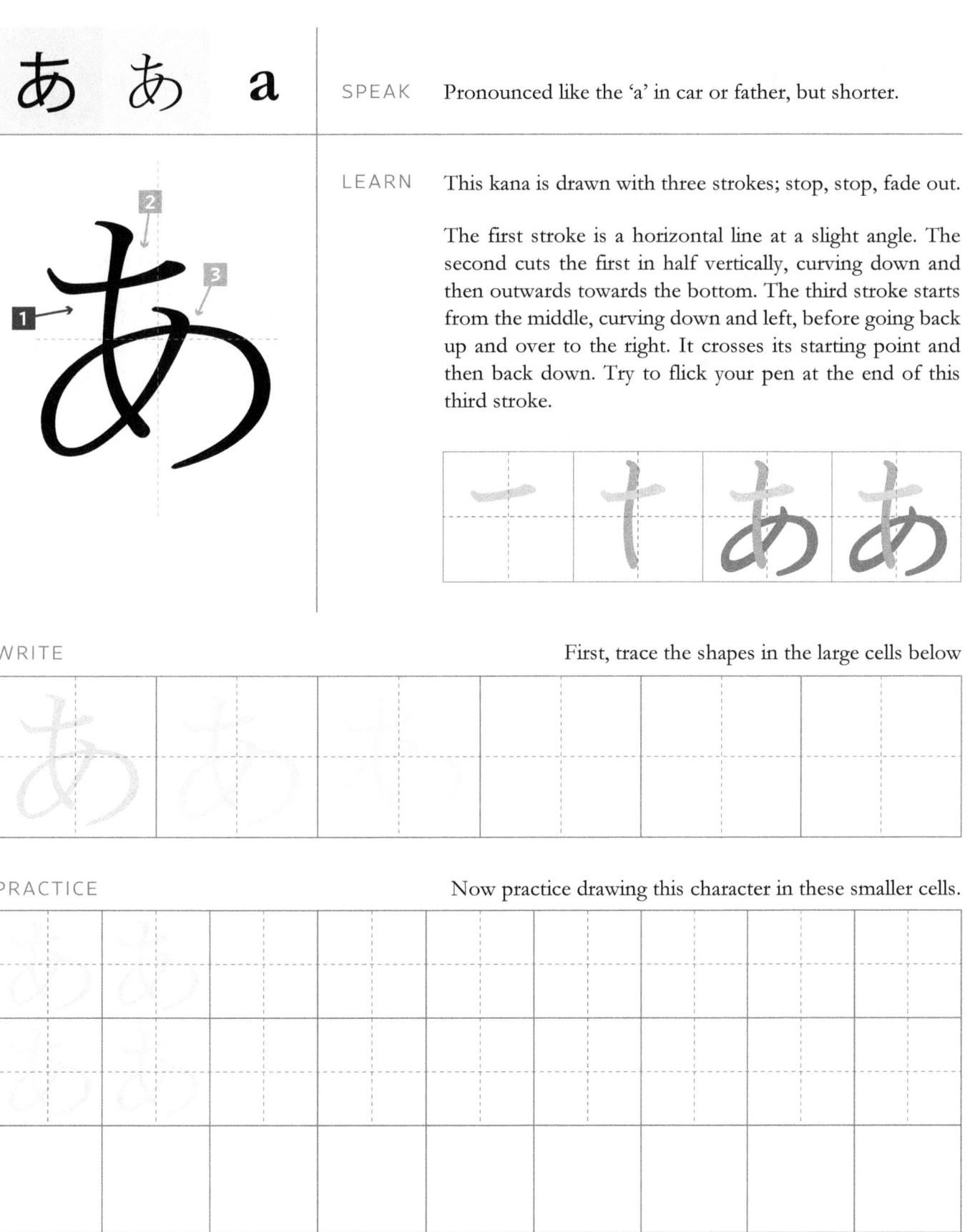

WRITE — First, trace the shapes in the large cells below

PRACTICE — Now practice drawing this character in these smaller cells.

い　い　i

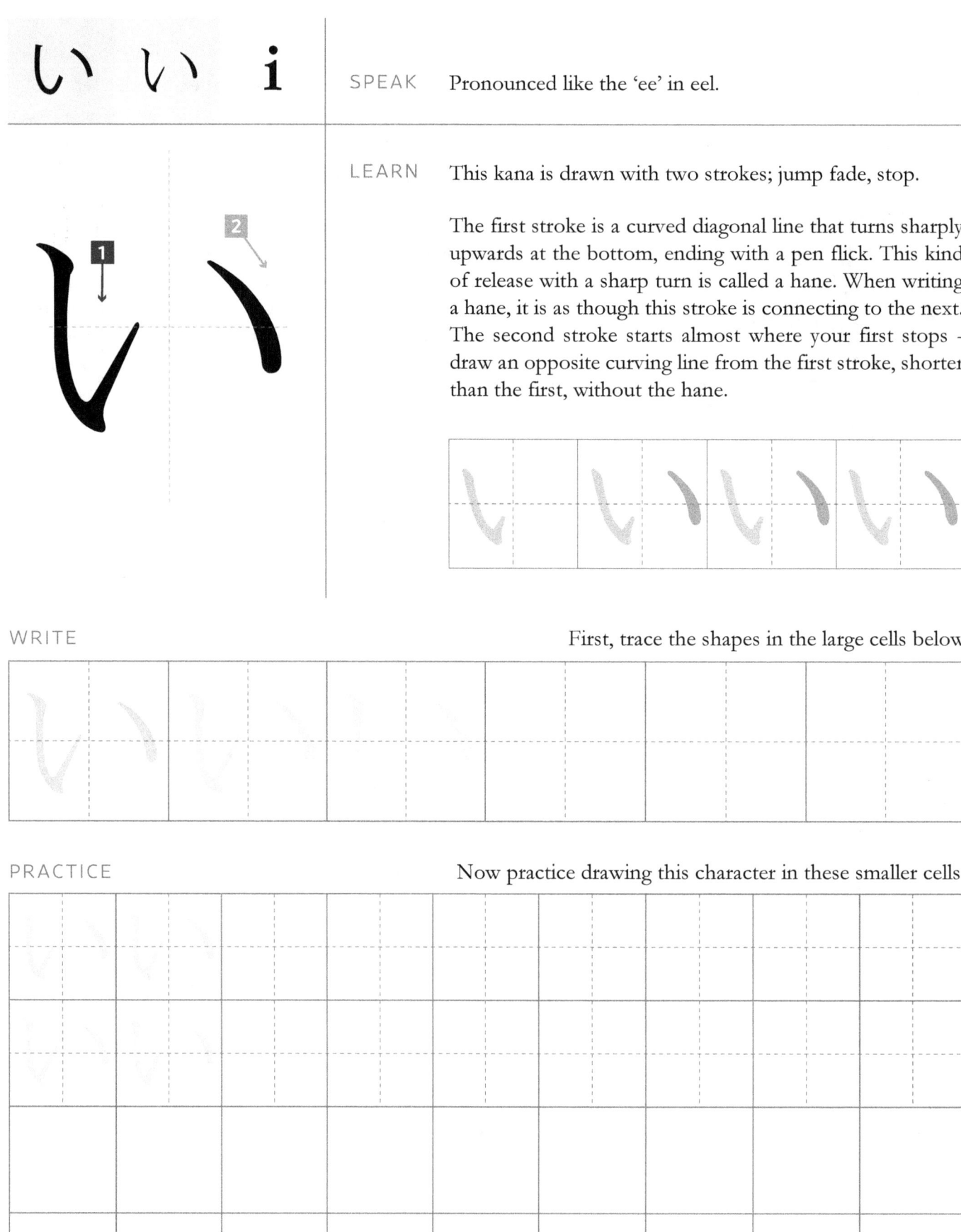

SPEAK　Pronounced like the 'ee' in eel.

LEARN　This kana is drawn with two strokes; jump fade, stop.

The first stroke is a curved diagonal line that turns sharply upwards at the bottom, ending with a pen flick. This kind of release with a sharp turn is called a hane. When writing a hane, it is as though this stroke is connecting to the next. The second stroke starts almost where your first stops - draw an opposite curving line from the first stroke, shorter than the first, without the hane.

WRITE　First, trace the shapes in the large cells below

PRACTICE　Now practice drawing this character in these smaller cells.

| う | う | **u** |

SPEAK — Pronounced like the 'oo' in zoo.

LEARN — This kana is drawn with two strokes; jump fade, stop.

Draw the short slanted line at the top center, and flick your pen back and away to the left. Be mindful of the second stroke as you flick the pen away - it begins almost where the first ended, in the same direction. The ear shape curves up to the right and then down to the bottom center. Flick your pen as you complete this stroke too. The first stroke doesn't want to be too big or it will look off balance.

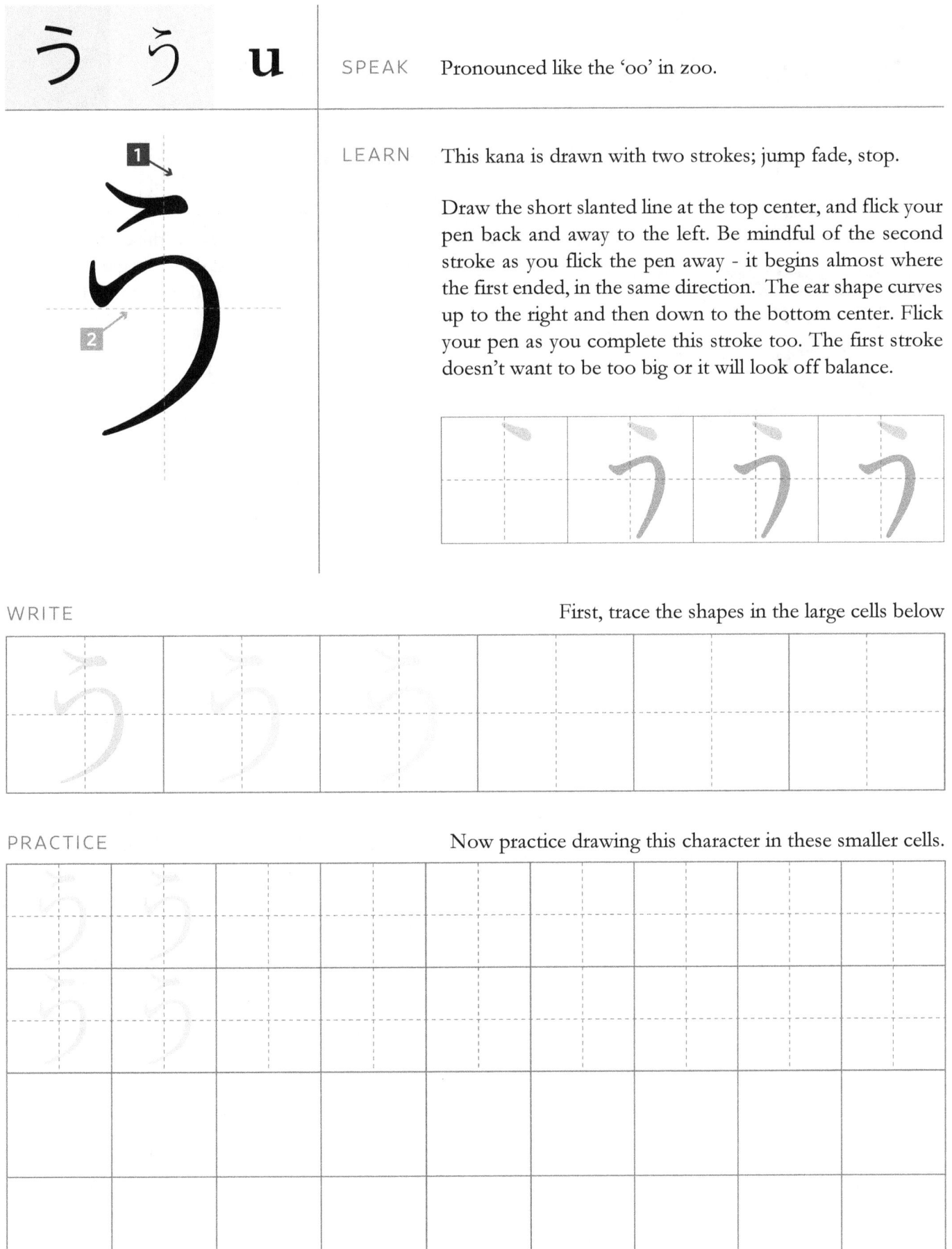

WRITE — First, trace the shapes in the large cells below

PRACTICE — Now practice drawing this character in these smaller cells.

17

| え え **e** | SPEAK | Pronounced as 'eh' like the 'e' in men. |

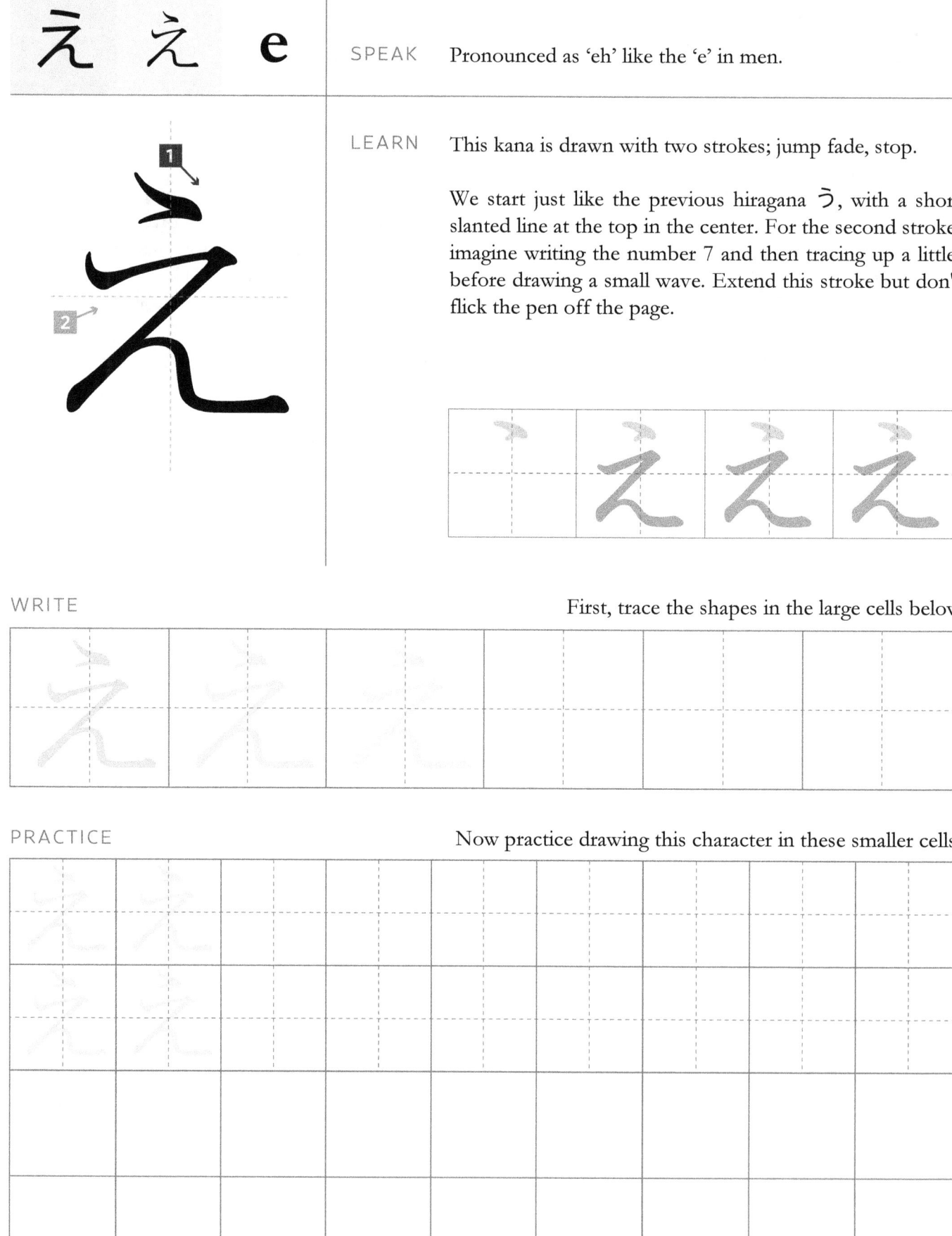

LEARN — This kana is drawn with two strokes; jump fade, stop.

We start just like the previous hiragana う, with a short slanted line at the top in the center. For the second stroke, imagine writing the number 7 and then tracing up a little, before drawing a small wave. Extend this stroke but don't flick the pen off the page.

WRITE — First, trace the shapes in the large cells below

PRACTICE — Now practice drawing this character in these smaller cells.

 **o**

SPEAK   Pronounced like the 'o' in original.

LEARN   This kana is drawn with three strokes; stop, fade, stop.

Start with a short horizontal line, just as with あ, but a little lower and to the left. The second stroke cuts the first in half with a vertical line, turning sharply to the left at the bottom. It then turns again to create a large curve before flicking your pen off at the end. The third small stroke positioned up to the top right of the first stroke.

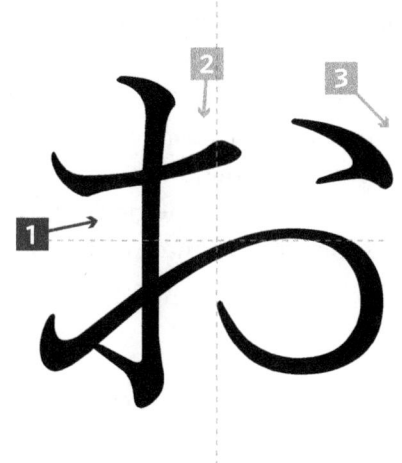

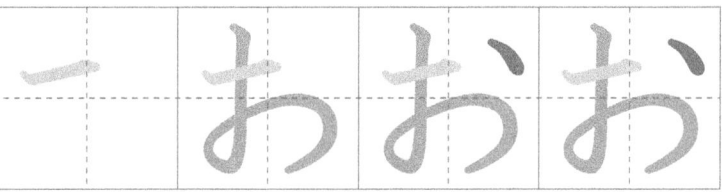

WRITE   First, trace the shapes in the large cells below

PRACTICE   Now practice drawing this character in these smaller cells.

19

か か **ka**

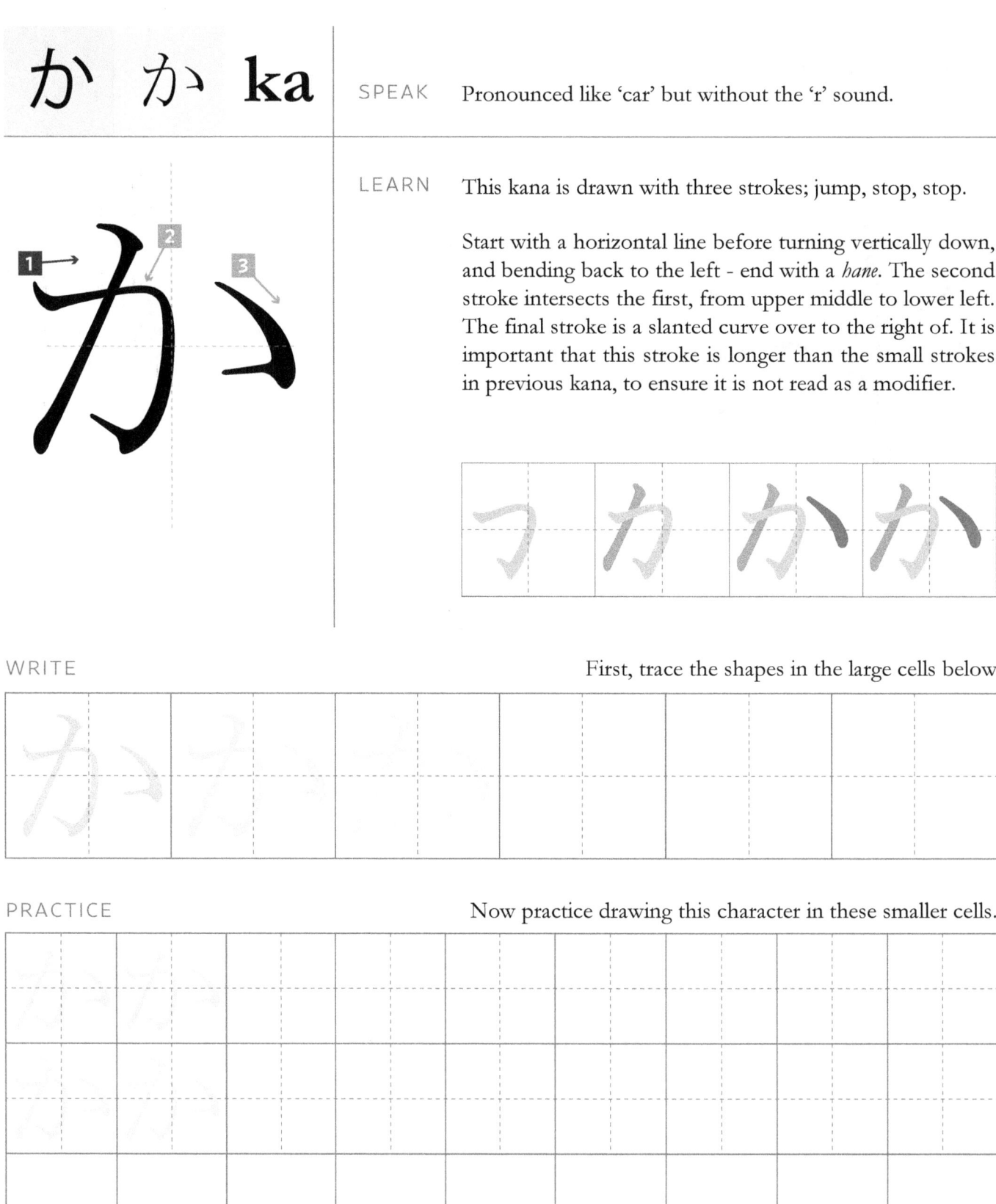

SPEAK — Pronounced like 'car' but without the 'r' sound.

LEARN — This kana is drawn with three strokes; jump, stop, stop.

Start with a horizontal line before turning vertically down, and bending back to the left - end with a *hane*. The second stroke intersects the first, from upper middle to lower left. The final stroke is a slanted curve over to the right of. It is important that this stroke is longer than the small strokes in previous kana, to ensure it is not read as a modifier.

WRITE — First, trace the shapes in the large cells below

PRACTICE — Now practice drawing this character in these smaller cells.

き き **ki**

SPEAK — Pronounced like 'key'.

LEARN — Drawn with four strokes; stop, stop, jump fade, stop.

Your first two strokes are parallel lines, from left to right, and at a slight angle. Stroke three cuts through the first two, and ends with a *hane*. Draw your hane moving upwards, setting up the fourth mark. Draw the last curved stop mark around to the right. You often see these marks connected in some fonts, as shown in the small image on the left, but this is the correct way to draw this character.

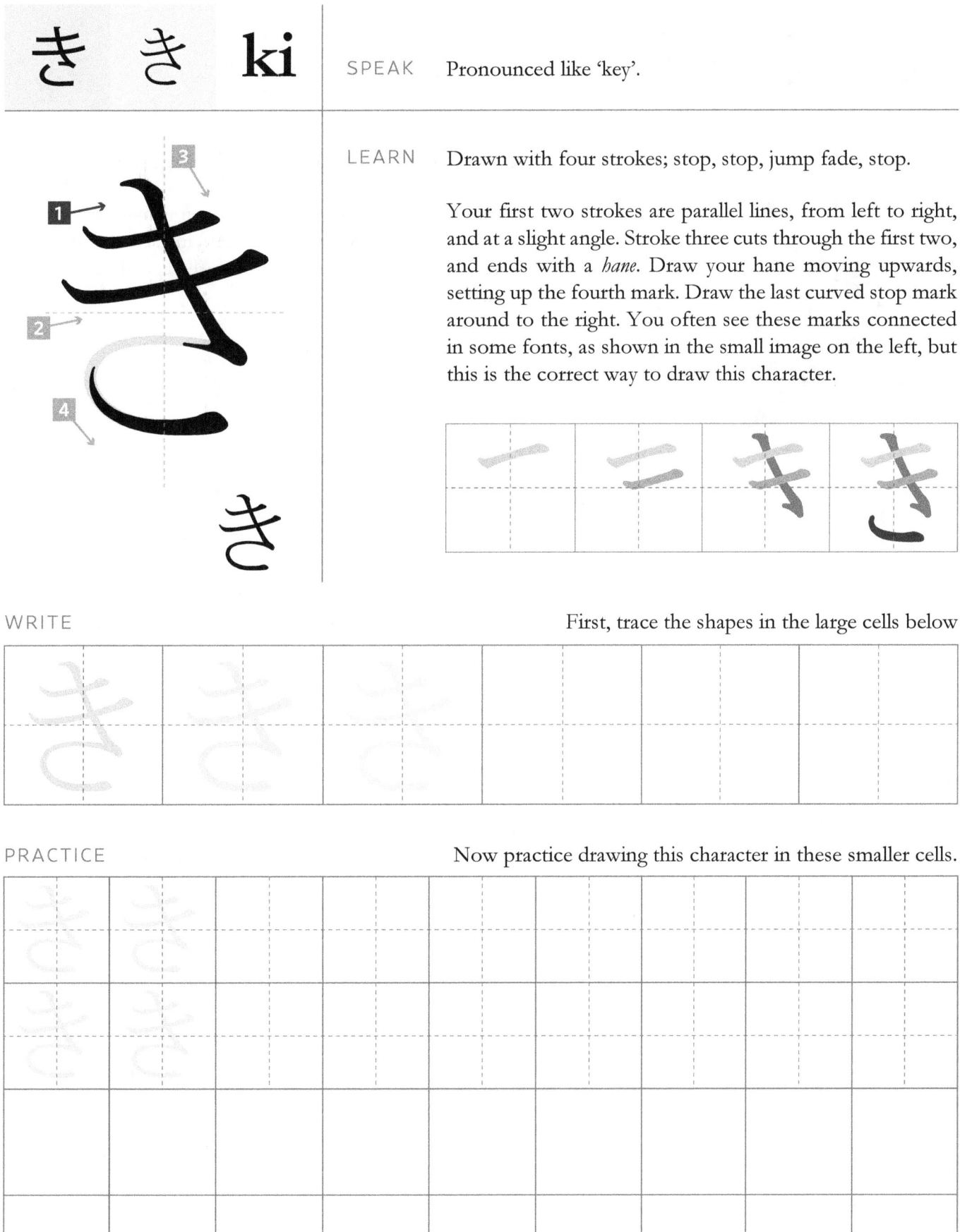

WRITE — First, trace the shapes in the large cells below

PRACTICE — Now practice drawing this character in these smaller cells.

く く **ku**

SPEAK — Pronounced like the 'koo' in cuckoo.

LEARN — This kana is drawn with just one stroke: a stop.

This single stroke character is drawn much like an opening angle bracket, but with a slight bend inwards. Try to make sure that the start and end points are aligned vertically, to create a neat balanced character.

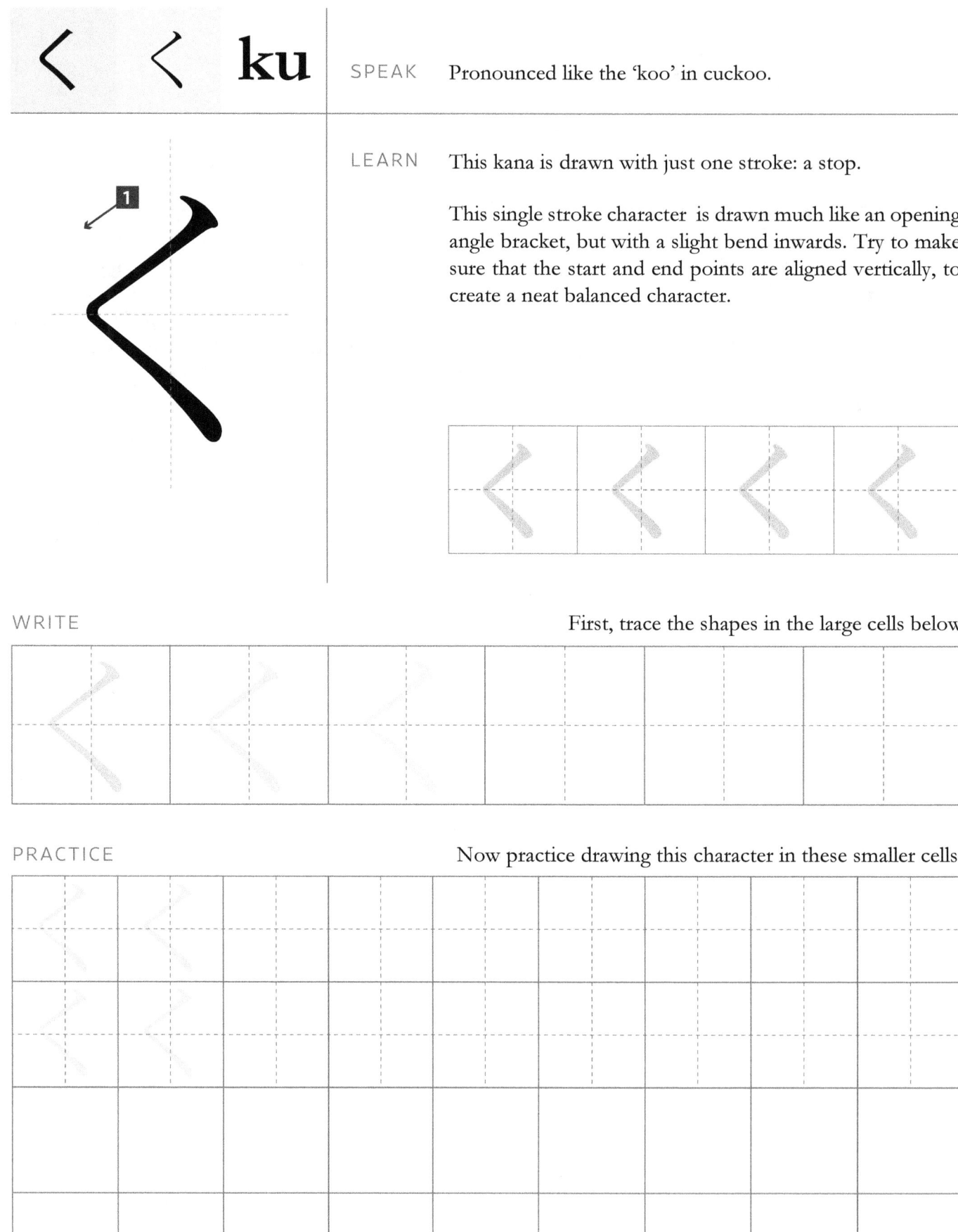

WRITE — First, trace the shapes in the large cells below

PRACTICE — Now practice drawing this character in these smaller cells.

け け **ke**

SPEAK   Pronounced like the 'ke' in Kenneth

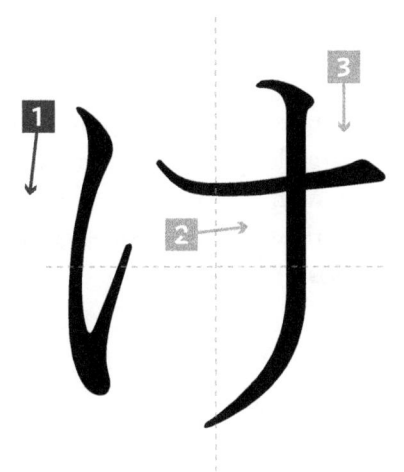

LEARN   This kana has three strokes: a jump fade, a stop, and a fade.

Draw the first stroke downwards with a bit of a curve outwards and ending with a hane. The second mark is made as a continuation from the hane, with a short line left to right. Your last stroke is another vertical line down, with a curve to the left this time. It starts a little higher than before, and ends lower too. Finish this stroke with a flick of your pen.

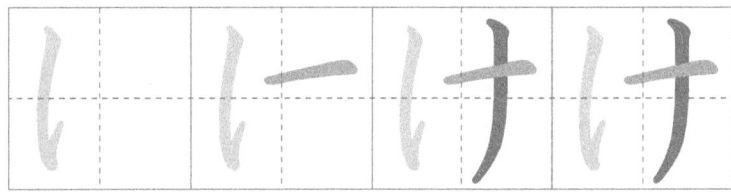

WRITE   First, trace the shapes in the large cells below

PRACTICE   Now practice drawing this character in these smaller cells.

23

こ ko

SPEAK — Pronounced like the 'co' in core

LEARN — This kana is drawn with two strokes: a jump and a stop.

Draw this kana is with two strokes that curve inwards almost connecting to make a large loop. The first mark is a curved horizontal line ending with a hane. Your second stroke starts lower down and to the left. The strokes should look as though they are almost connecting to create a closed circular shape.

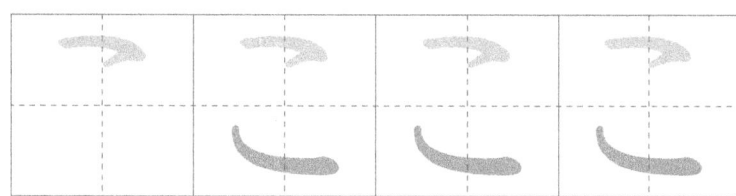

WRITE — First, trace the shapes in the large cells below

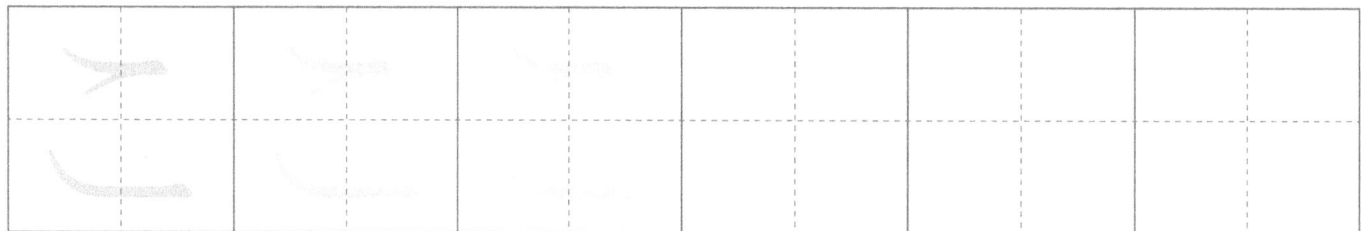

PRACTICE — Now practice drawing this character in these smaller cells.

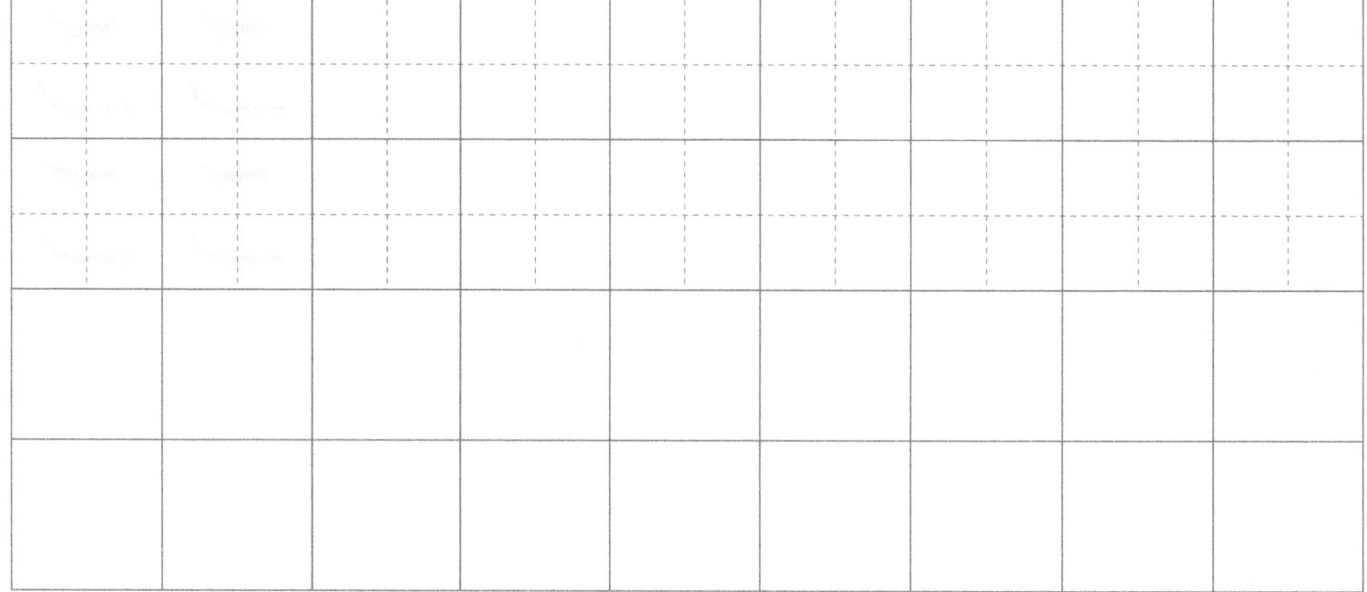

さ　さ　**sa**

SPEAK　Pronounced like the 'sa' in sardines.

LEARN　This kana is drawn with three strokes: stop, jump, stop

Written in a similar way to き but without the first short stroke. Start with the angled horizontal line from left to right. Your second stroke cuts through this mark and ends with a hane. The third mark is made by putting your pen down slightly after the hane and curving back around. This kana is often displayed as being connected but the correct method is to lift your pen.

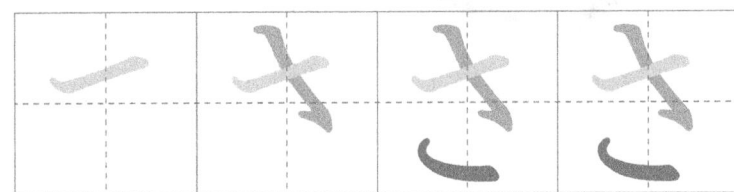

WRITE　First, trace the shapes in the large cells below

PRACTICE　Now practice drawing this character in these smaller cells.

25

し　し　shi

SPEAK — Pronounced like 'she' as in sheet.

LEARN — Draw this kana with a single stroke; a brushed fade.

This kana is written with just one stroke. It begins as a vertical line from top to bottom before curving out to the right and upwards. Flick your pen from the page at the end.

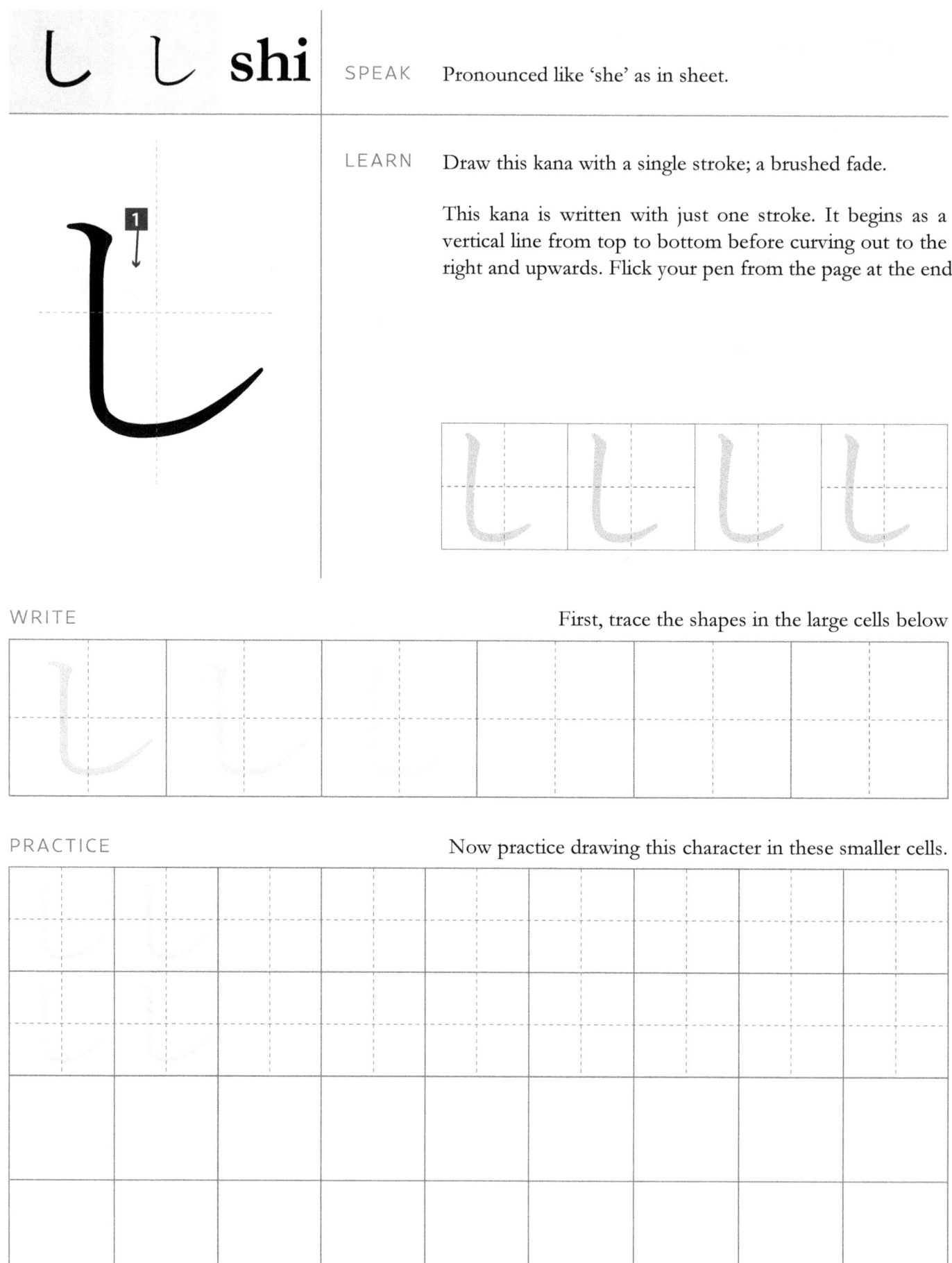

WRITE — First, trace the shapes in the large cells below

PRACTICE — Now practice drawing this character in these smaller cells.

す　す　su

SPEAK　Pronounced like the 'su' in super

LEARN　This has two strokes; a stop, and a looping fade.

Begin with a long line drawn from left to right. Your second mark starts at the top and is drawn down through the first. It then creates a loop just after the intersection. Complete the stroke by curving down to the left and flick your pen from the paper at the end to fade the stroke out. Try to cut through the first stroke slightly off center, to the right. This will create more space for your loop below.

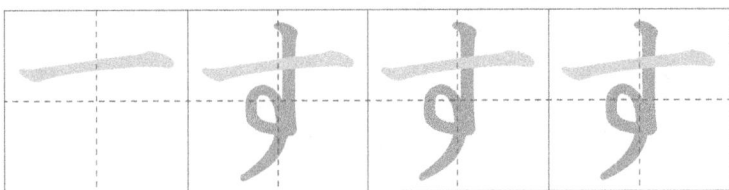

WRITE　　　　　　　　　　　　　　First, trace the shapes in the large cells below

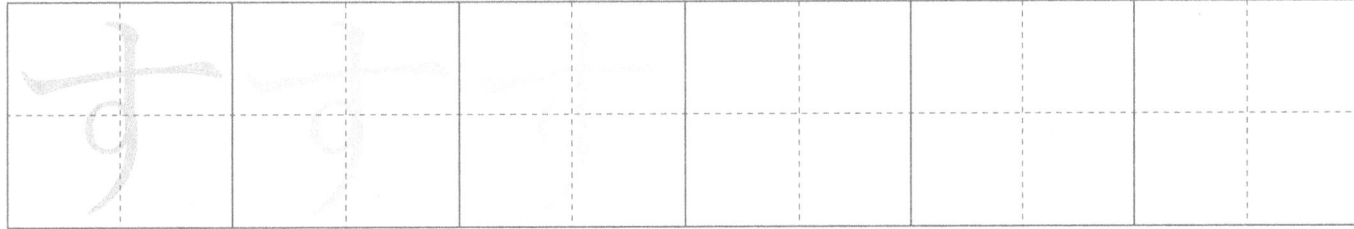

PRACTICE　　　　　　　　　　　Now practice drawing this character in these smaller cells.

せ せ **se**

SPEAK   Pronounced like 'say' but with less 'y'.

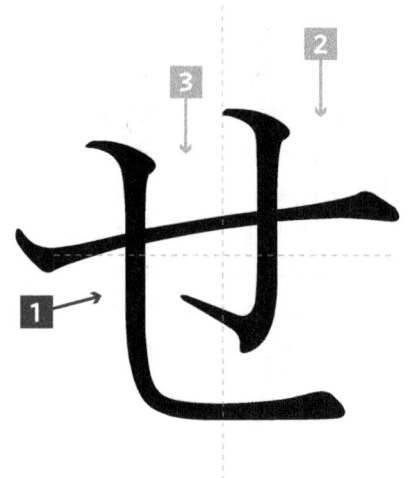

LEARN   This kana is drawn with three strokes; stop, jump, stop

Begin this character with a long horizontal line, left to right. The second stroke is a shorter, vertical line to the right side and ends with a hane upwards and left. Lift your pen but keep momentum in the same direction as you set up for the third stroke. Make a vertical line down and bend around and to the right. Don't flick your pen here. The first two marks should cut through the first with even spaces.

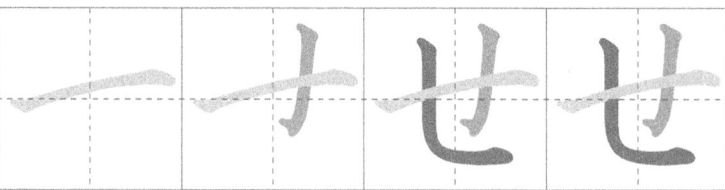

WRITE   First, trace the shapes in the large cells below

PRACTICE   Now practice drawing this character in these smaller cells.

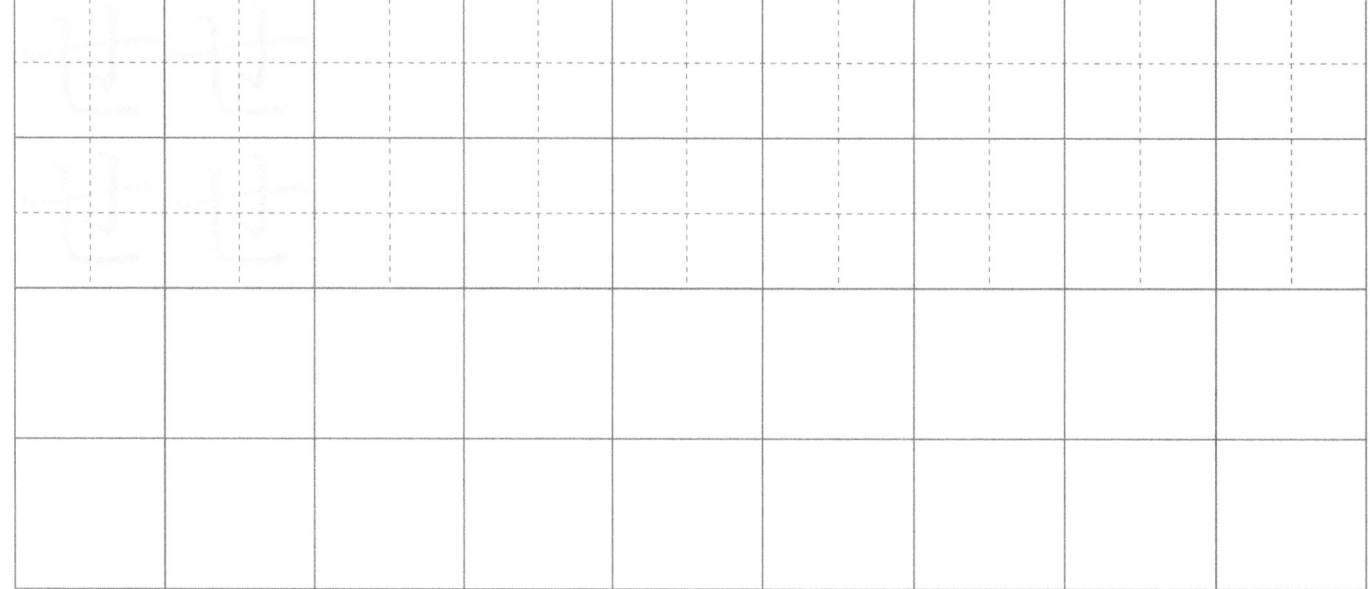

そ そ **so**

SPEAK   Pronounced like the 'so' in soy.

LEARN   This kana is created with a single zig-zag stroke; stop.

Start by making the 'Z' shape in the top half, before adding the 'C' shape below - don't lift your pen from the page. The 'C' shape should end without any upwards motion. Make sure that your middle horizontal line is longer than the top one. Whilst rare, you may see this character displayed as two strokes in some fonts.

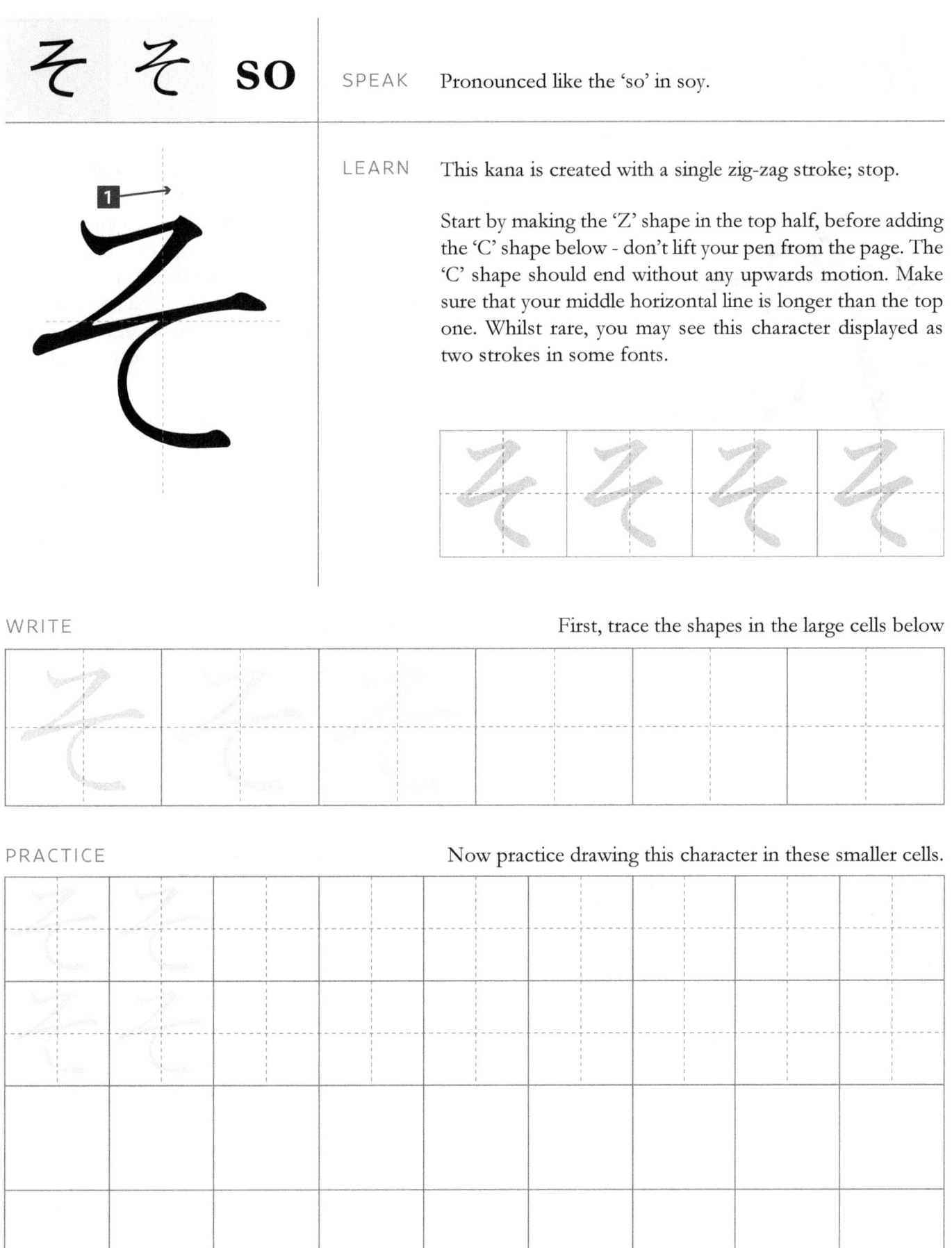

WRITE   First, trace the shapes in the large cells below

PRACTICE   Now practice drawing this character in these smaller cells.

た た **ta**

SPEAK Pronounced like the 'ta' in target.

LEARN This kana is drawn with four strokes; they are all stops.

Make a lower case 't' shape, with the vertical line pointing down and left. Make this in the left half of the cell, so there is room for the next part. Your third stroke creates a small curved mark to the right of the T shape and stroke four is made below, with an opposite curve to the previous stroke. The final two strokes should look like they are almost connecting to make a circular shape.

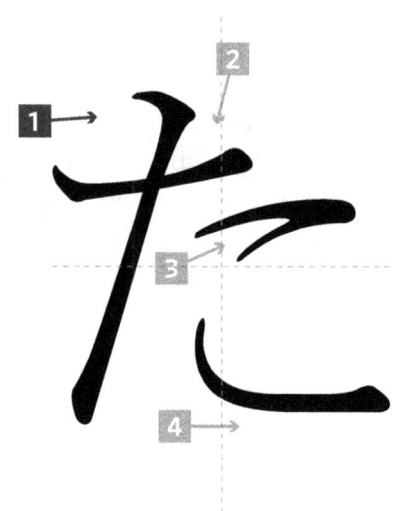

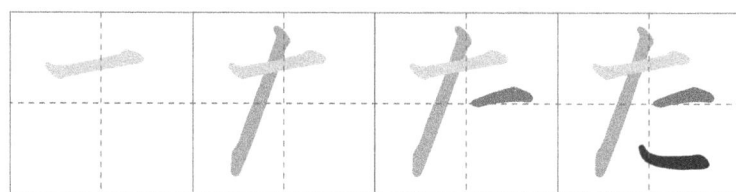

WRITE First, trace the shapes in the large cells below

PRACTICE Now practice drawing this character in these smaller cells.

ち ち chi

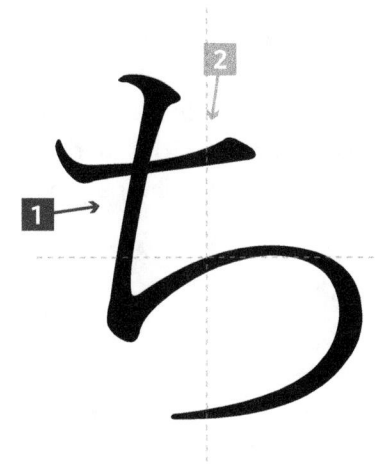

SPEAK   Pronounced just like the 'chi' in tai-chi.

LEARN   This kana is drawn with two strokes; stop, fade.

We write this character as a mirror image of さ, but there is no need to lift your pen. Draw your first mark from left to right, at a slight angle. Your second stroke is a slightly diagonal line down and to the left, intersecting with the first. As you approach the bottom, it curves back up and around to the right, making a circular shape and ending with a flick from the page.

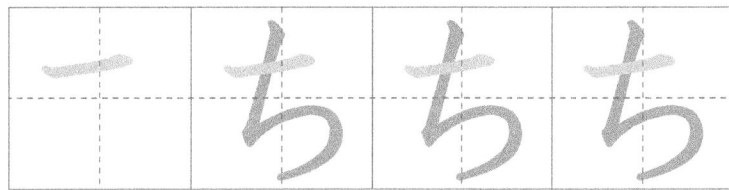

WRITE   First, trace the shapes in the large cells below

PRACTICE   Now practice drawing this character in these smaller cells.

つ つ **tsu**

SPEAK — Pronounced just as the 'tsu' in tsunami, with a silent 't'.

LEARN — This kana is drawn with just a single stroke; fade.

As one of the most simple characters, this kana is made with one long, sweeping curve that fades out at the end. Create the fade by flicking your pen from the page as you approach the end of the arc.

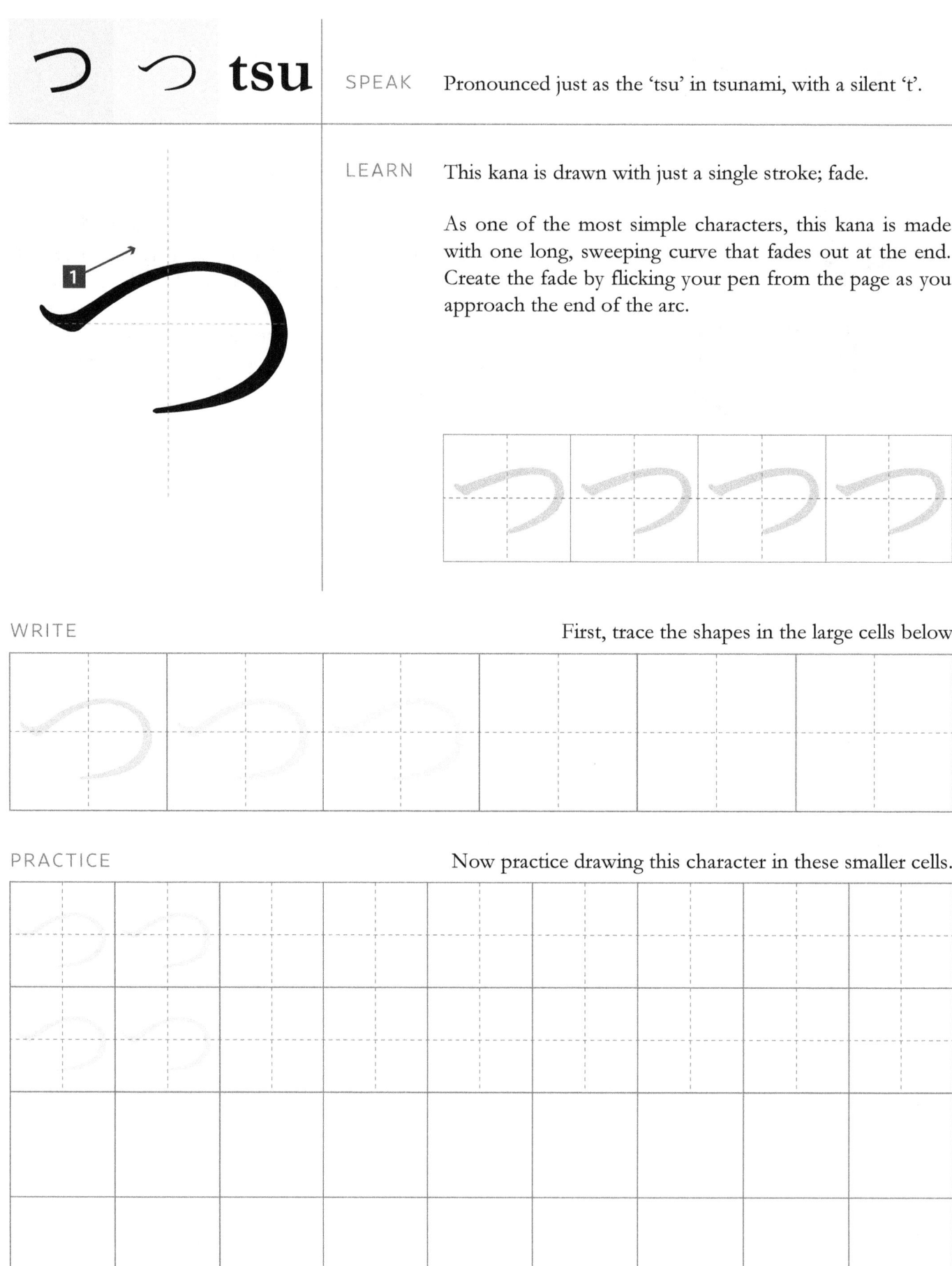

WRITE — First, trace the shapes in the large cells below

PRACTICE — Now practice drawing this character in these smaller cells.

て て **te**

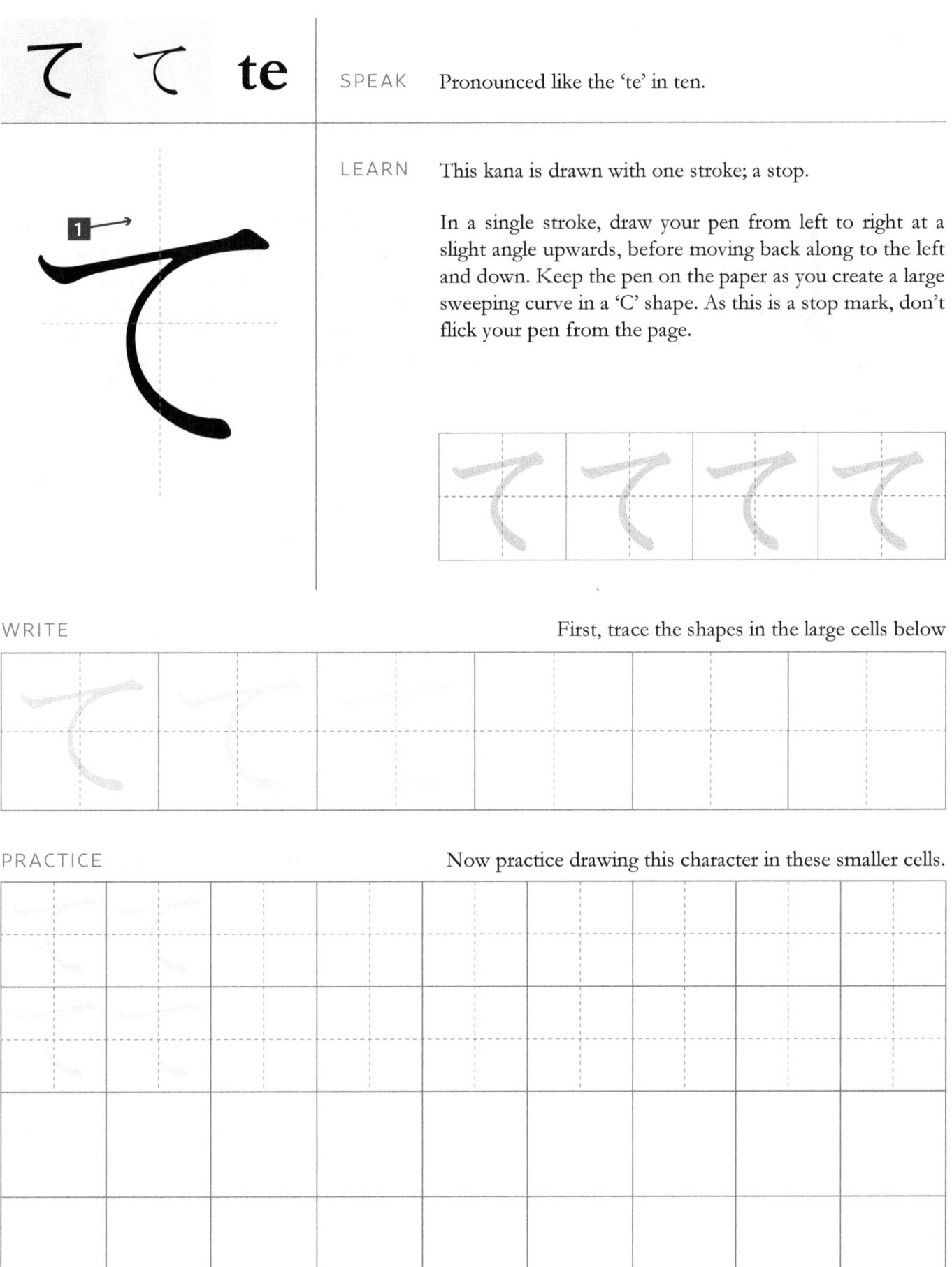

SPEAK — Pronounced like the 'te' in ten.

LEARN — This kana is drawn with one stroke; a stop.

In a single stroke, draw your pen from left to right at a slight angle upwards, before moving back along to the left and down. Keep the pen on the paper as you create a large sweeping curve in a 'C' shape. As this is a stop mark, don't flick your pen from the page.

WRITE — First, trace the shapes in the large cells below

PRACTICE — Now practice drawing this character in these smaller cells.

と と **to**

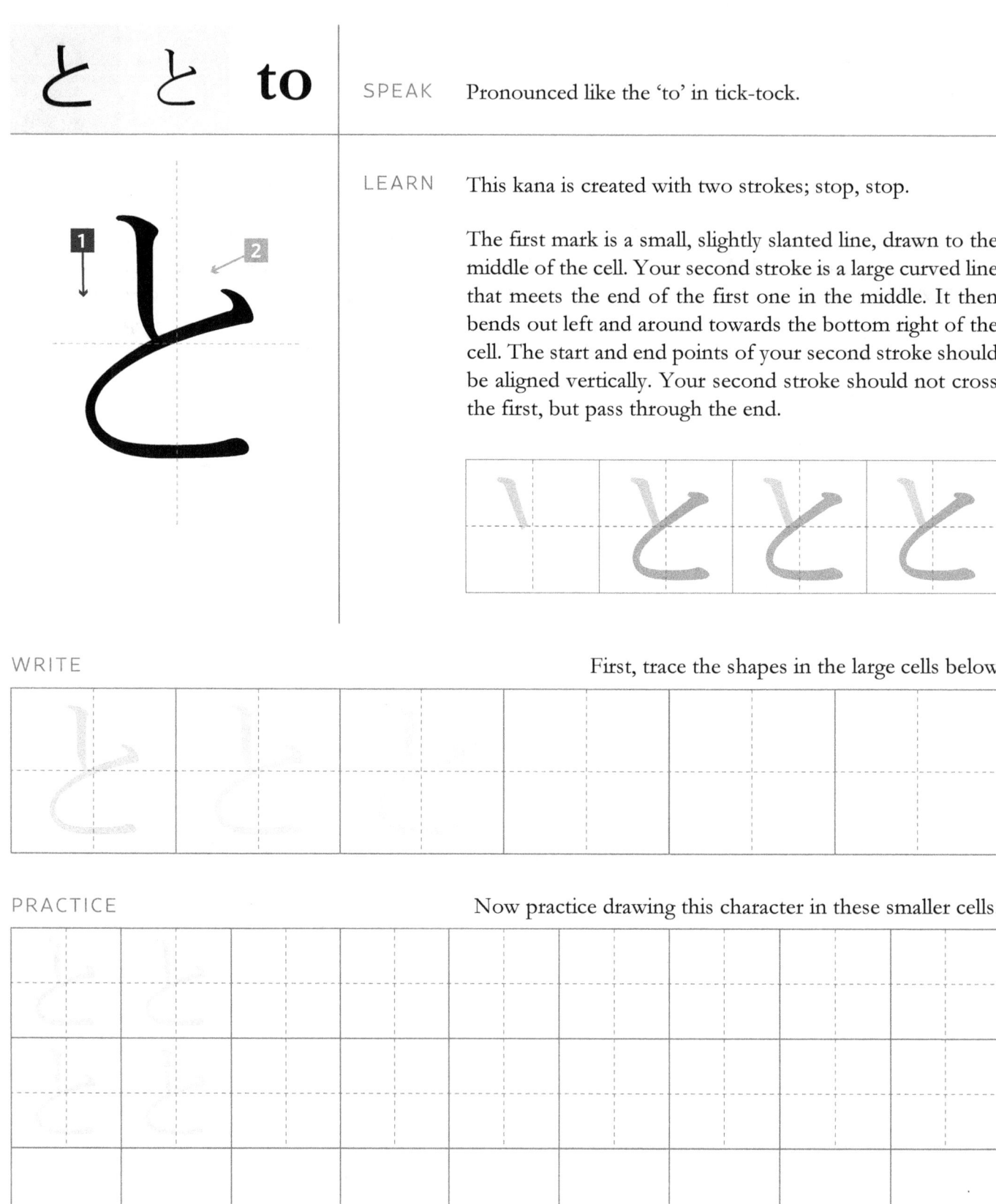

SPEAK — Pronounced like the 'to' in tick-tock.

LEARN — This kana is created with two strokes; stop, stop.

The first mark is a small, slightly slanted line, drawn to the middle of the cell. Your second stroke is a large curved line that meets the end of the first one in the middle. It then bends out left and around towards the bottom right of the cell. The start and end points of your second stroke should be aligned vertically. Your second stroke should not cross the first, but pass through the end.

WRITE — First, trace the shapes in the large cells below

PRACTICE — Now practice drawing this character in these smaller cells.

な な **na**

SPEAK Pronounced like the 'na' in narwhal.

LEARN This kana has four strokes; stop, stop, jump fade, and stop.

Begin with a short, angled horizontal line on the left. Your second mark is a longer diagonal stroke cutting through the first, down and left - don't make it too long. The third stroke is made as a curved line on the right side, ending with a hane. Just as you lift your pen, immediately start the fourth stroke downwards before looping over itself. End this loop with a stop below the third stroke.

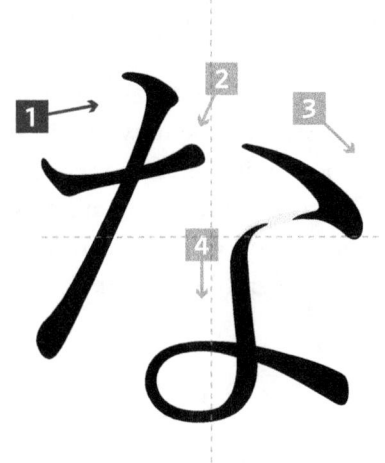

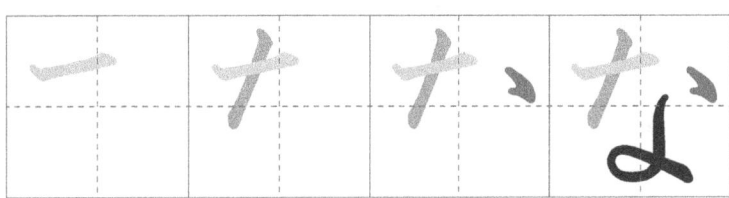

WRITE First, trace the shapes in the large cells below

PRACTICE Now practice drawing this character in these smaller cells.

35

に に **ni**

SPEAK — Pronounced like the 'nee' in needle, but shorter.

LEARN — This kana has three strokes; a jump fade, and two stops.

Much like previous characters, begin with a vertical line down on the left side, and end with a hane upwards to the right. Your second mark is almost a continuation from the hane, and is a small curved horizontal line. The last mark is made as a curve in the opposite direction, almost making a circle. Don't flick your pen off the end here, as it is a stop mark.

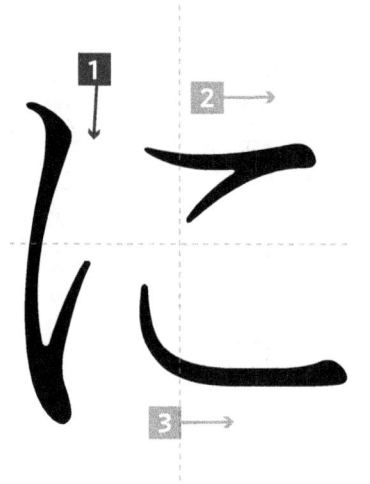

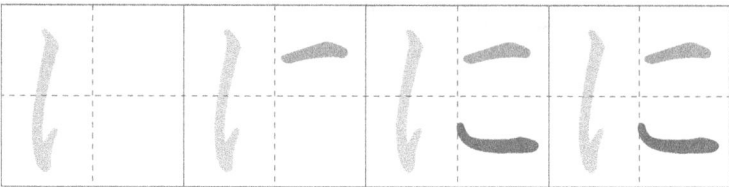

WRITE — First, trace the shapes in the large cells below

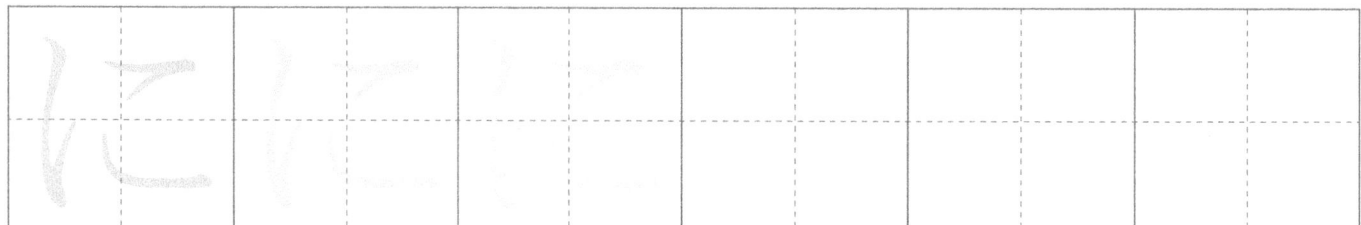

PRACTICE — Now practice drawing this character in these smaller cells.

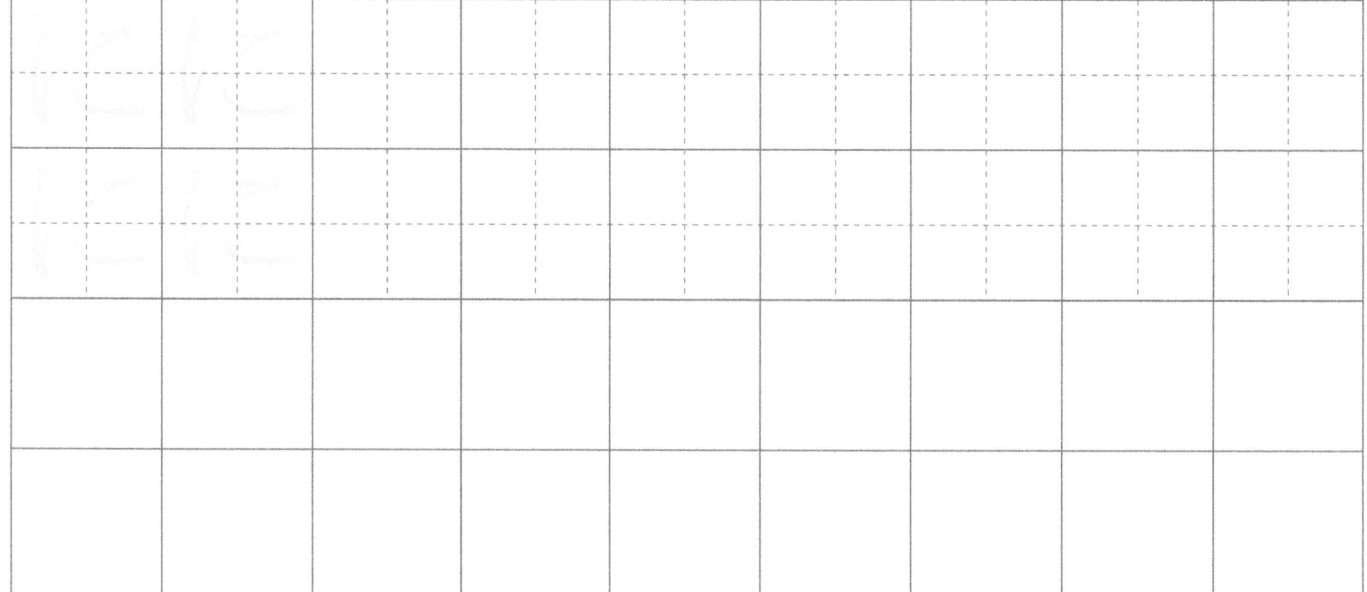

ぬ ぬ **nu**

SPEAK — Pronounced like the 'noo' in noodles but short.

LEARN — Drawn with two strokes; a stop and a long looping stop.

Start by drawing a slightly curved line at an angle. Your second mark begins at a similar sort of height, but curves back towards the first. It then loops up and back over to the right. As your pen approaches the lower right of the cell, loop back over and to the right. Take care to match the spaces between the lines in the example so that your character is well-balanced.

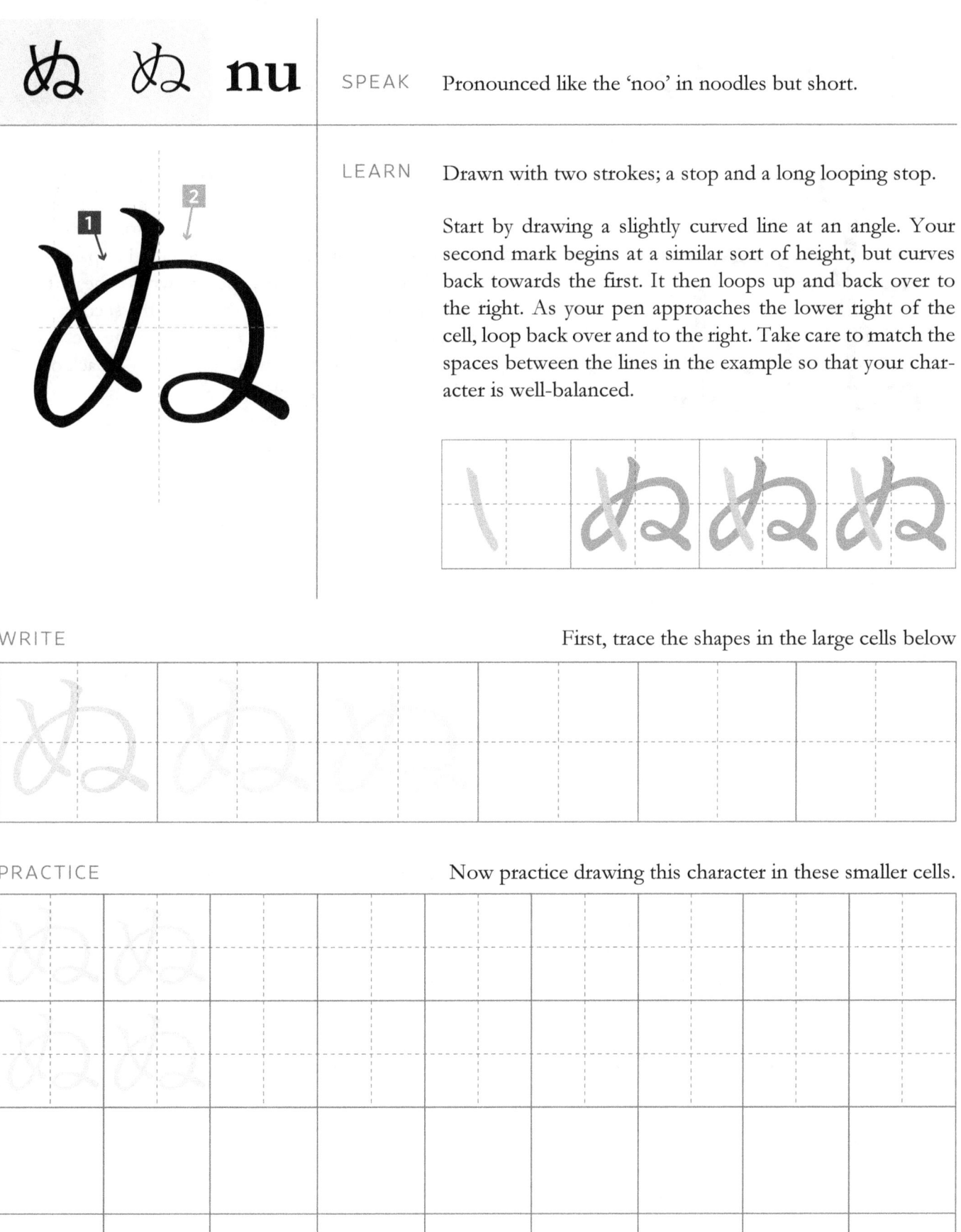

WRITE — First, trace the shapes in the large cells below

PRACTICE — Now practice drawing this character in these smaller cells.

37

ね ね **ne**

SPEAK — Pronounced like the 'ne' in nest.

LEARN — This kana is drawn with two strokes; stop, long stop.

Draw the vertical line from top to bottom. Start your second stroke with a short horizontal line that passes over the first, before moving your pen down to the left side. Without taking your pen from the page, the second stroke returns upward and continues to create a large arc. As you approach the bottom right, make a small loop back over to the right to complete the character.

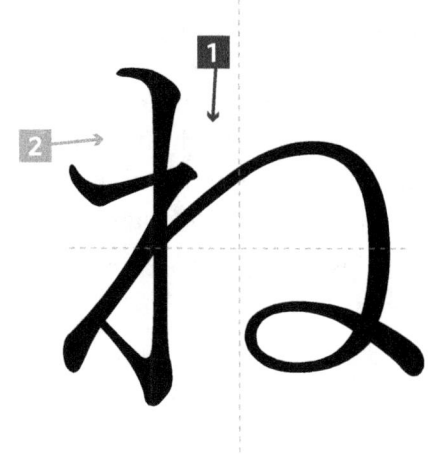

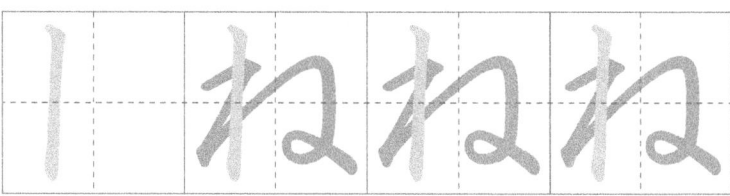

WRITE — First, trace the shapes in the large cells below

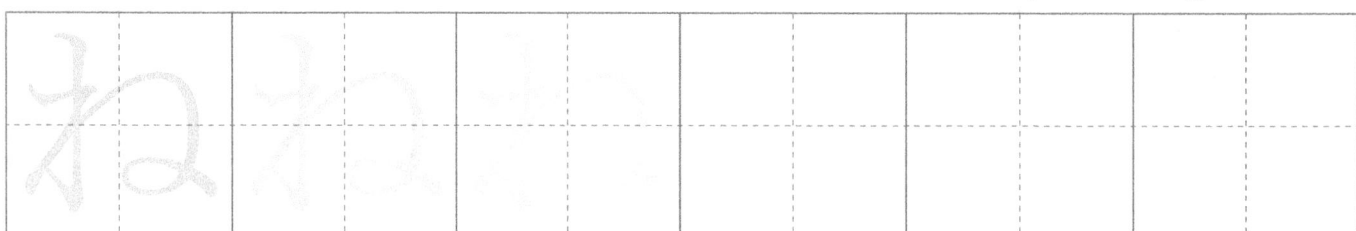

PRACTICE — Now practice drawing this character in these smaller cells.

の の **no**

SPEAK — Pronounced like the 'no' in nose.

LEARN — This kana is written with one stroke; a long fade.

Starting from the upper center part of the cell, draw your pen down and diagonally to the left. From the bottom of this line, move your pen up and over to the right in a large circular motion, passing through the point you started from. When passing across your start point, be sure not to draw your curve too low and allow the vertical line to protrude above. Bring the arc around and flick your pen.

WRITE — First, trace the shapes in the large cells below

PRACTICE — Now practice drawing this character in these smaller cells.

39

は は **ha**

SPEAK | Pronounced as the 'ha' when laughing, like ha-ha.

LEARN | Draw this kana with three strokes; jump, stop, loop stop.

Your first two strokes will be similar to hiragana け, with a curved vertical stroke ending in a hane. The second stroke is a shorter horizontal line to the right. Your third stroke will pass through the second, drawn vertically downwards and ending with a small loop over itself to the right.

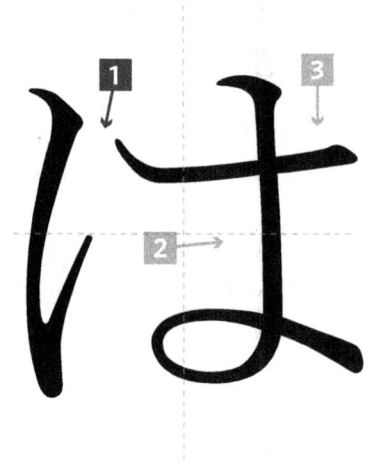

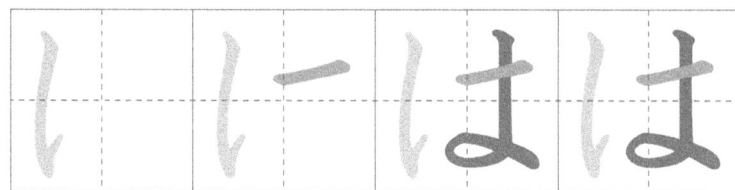

WRITE — First, trace the shapes in the large cells below

PRACTICE — Now practice drawing this character in these smaller cells.

ひ ひ hi

SPEAK Pronounced like the 'he' in He or She.

LEARN This kana is drawn with one stroke; a sweeping stop.

Start by making a short, slightly angled line up before returning back a little to the left. Keep your pen on the page as you create a large sweeping curve in a 'U' shape around the lower half of the cell. Once back near the top, and without lifting your pen, trace back a little and then away to the right with a curved line to a stop. Don't flick your pen from the paper here.

WRITE First, trace the shapes in the large cells below

PRACTICE Now practice drawing this character in these smaller cells.

41

SPEAK   Pronounced as 'hu' like the word 'who'.

LEARN   Drawn with four strokes; jump fade, jump, stop, and stop.

Begin with a short slanted stroke that ends with a hane at the top in the center. Your second stroke is then a sort of nose shape that should be ended with a flick towards the start of stroke three. This is another short slanted line ending with a hane, up and to the right. For the fourth, lift your pen to the right side where you draw the final, short curved line.

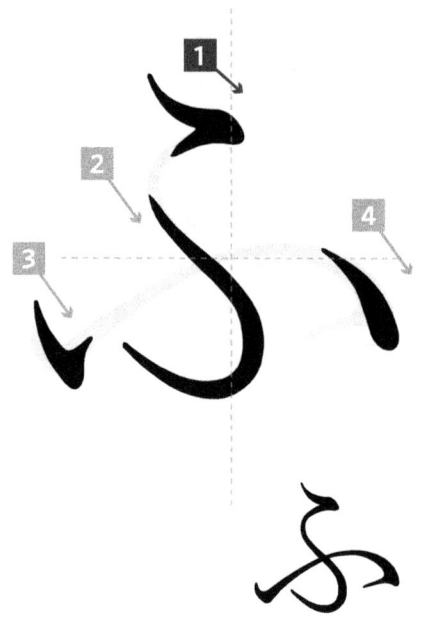

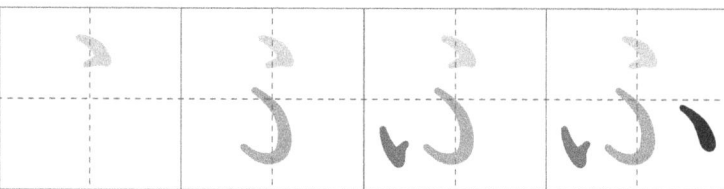

WRITE   First, trace the shapes in the large cells below

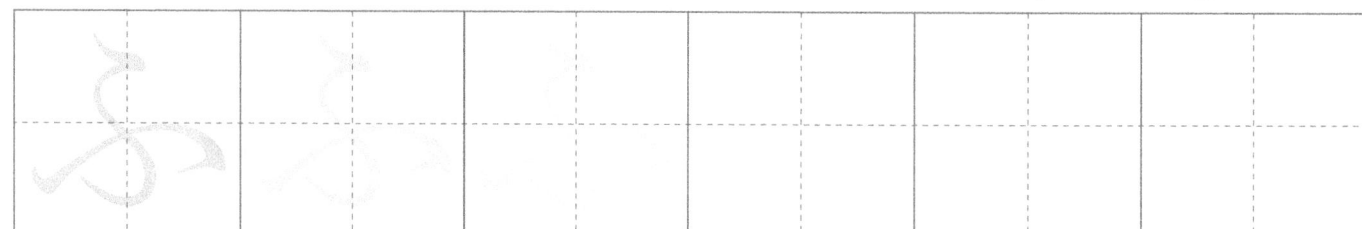

PRACTICE   Now practice drawing this character in these smaller cells.

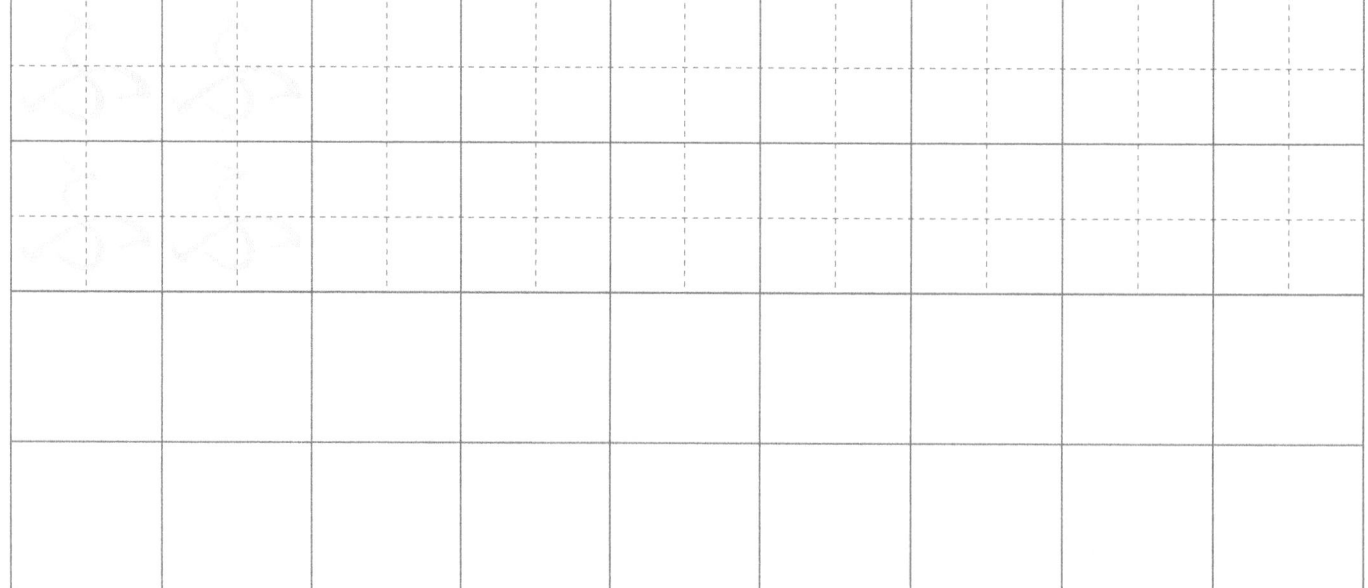

へ へ **he**

SPEAK Pronounced like the 'he' in Helen.

LEARN This kana is made with one stroke; a stop.

Start in the middle on the left of the cell and draw your pen diagonally up and right a short way - but don't pass across the center guideline. Without lifting your pen, continue to draw the longer diagonal line down and to the right. The 'top' of this inverted 'V' shape should not be in the center.

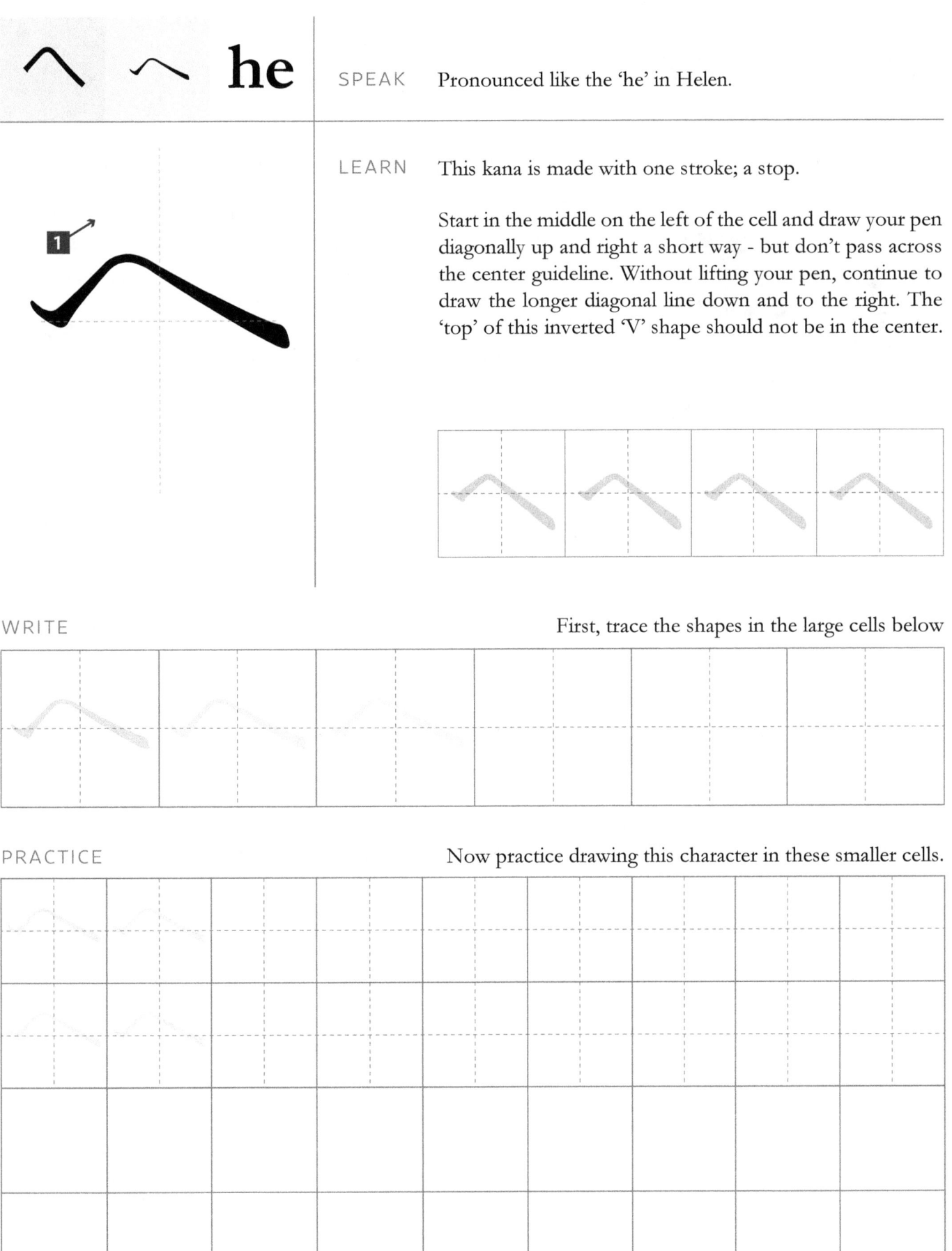

WRITE First, trace the shapes in the large cells below

PRACTICE Now practice drawing this character in these smaller cells.

ほ ほ ho

SPEAK Pronounced like the 'ho' in home.

LEARN This has four strokes; jump fade, stop, stop, loop stop.

Just as with the first strokes of は, に, and け, start with a curved vertical line that ends with a hane. Both the second and third strokes are short parallel lines in the upper right. Your final mark should start on the second line - be careful not to begin above it. Move your pen down, through the third stroke, and end with a loop back over your line to the right.

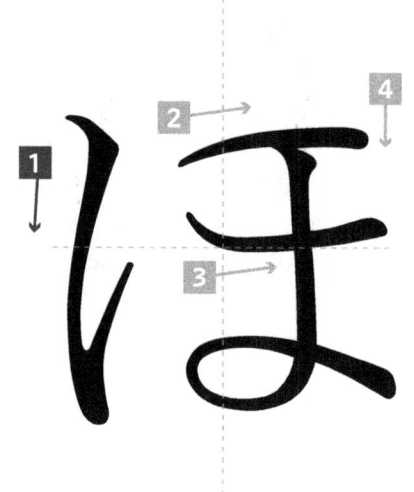

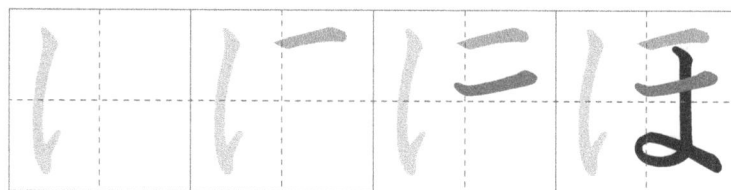

WRITE First, trace the shapes in the large cells below

PRACTICE Now practice drawing this character in these smaller cells.

ま ま **ma**

SPEAK — Pronounced like the 'ma' in market.

LEARN — Drawn with three strokes; stop, stop, looping stop.

Begin drawing this kana with parallel horizontal lines, both drawn from left to right. The first one should be a little longer than the second. Your third mark starts from the top, cuts through the first two strokes, and ends with a loop at the bottom. The key to accurately drawing this kana lies in not making the first strokes too long, yet still a little wider than the loop at the end.

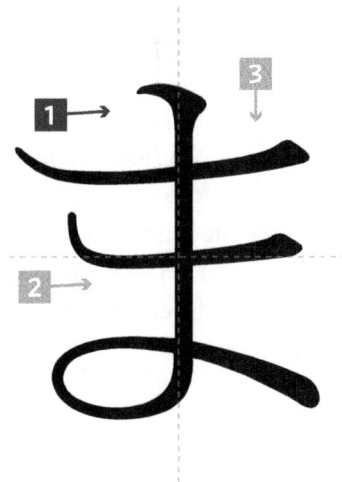

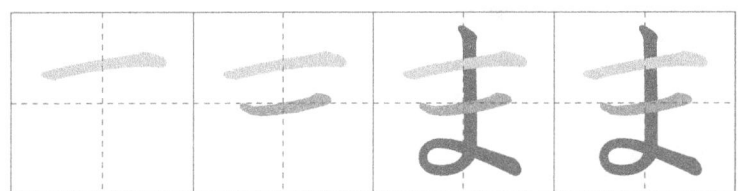

WRITE — First, trace the shapes in the large cells below

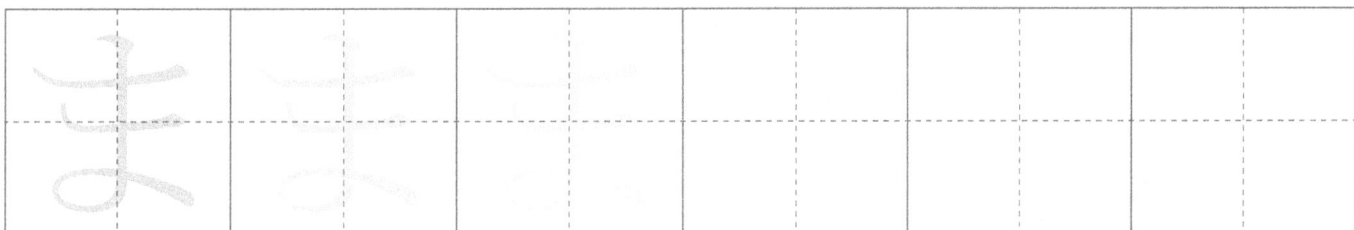

PRACTICE — Now practice drawing this character in these smaller cells.

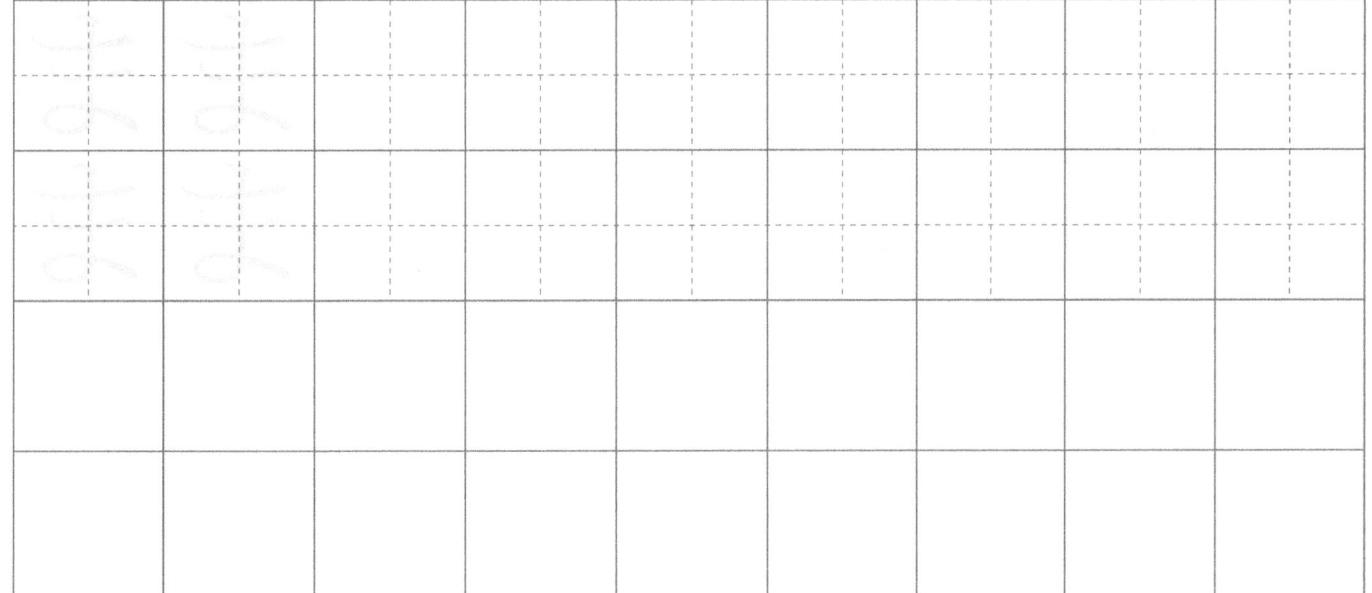

み み mi

SPEAK Pronounced just like 'me'.

LEARN Drawn with two strokes; long looping stop, and a fade.

Start your first stroke with a short horizontal line, then move your pen down and to the left. Without taking your pen from the page, make a loop at the bottom and finish the stroke with off with an arc to the right. Your second stroke is a curve, moving down and left, and cutting through the arc from the first stroke. Flick your pen from the page to fade this stroke out at the end.

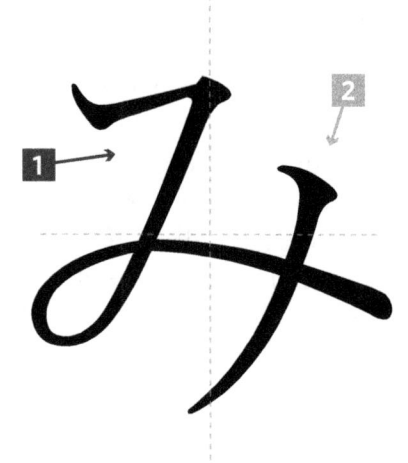

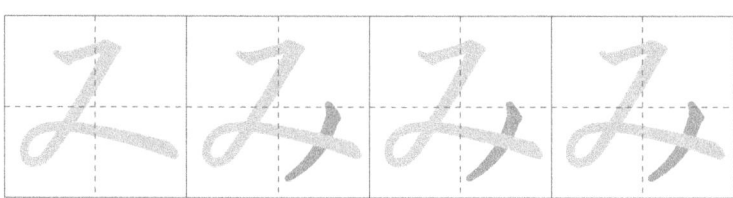

WRITE First, trace the shapes in the large cells below

PRACTICE Now practice drawing this character in these smaller cells.

む む mu

SPEAK Pronounced like 'moo' but in move.

LEARN Draw this kana with three strokes; stop, looping fade, stop.

We start drawing this kana in a similar way to す, with a horizontal line on the left side of the cell. The second mark begins at the top and is drawn down, through the first stroke, and then forms a loop below the center. Keeping your pen on the paper after the loop, draw down, across to the right, and then sharply up. Stop before going as high as the first stroke. Finish with a short slanted line.

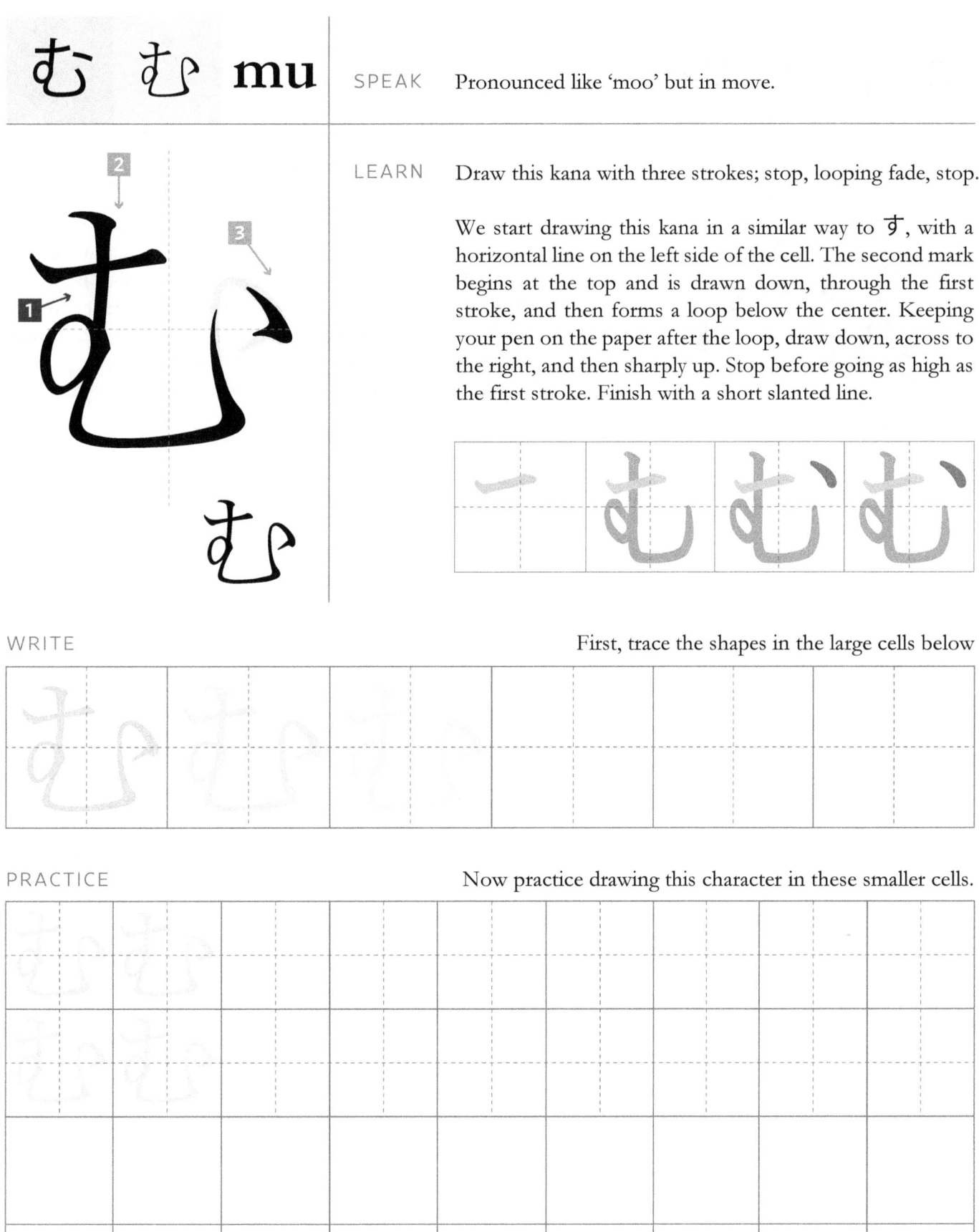

WRITE First, trace the shapes in the large cells below

PRACTICE Now practice drawing this character in these smaller cells.

め め **me**

SPEAK   Pronounced as 'meh' like the 'me' in mend.

LEARN   This kana is drawn with two strokes; stop, long fade.

We write this in a similar way to ぬ, except without a loop at the end. First, draw the curved diagonal line down and to the right. The second stroke begins at a similar height to the first, but curves the opposite way. Continue this stroke around in a large circular motion but flick your pen from the paper at the end. Try to match the spaces between lines to create an accurate character.

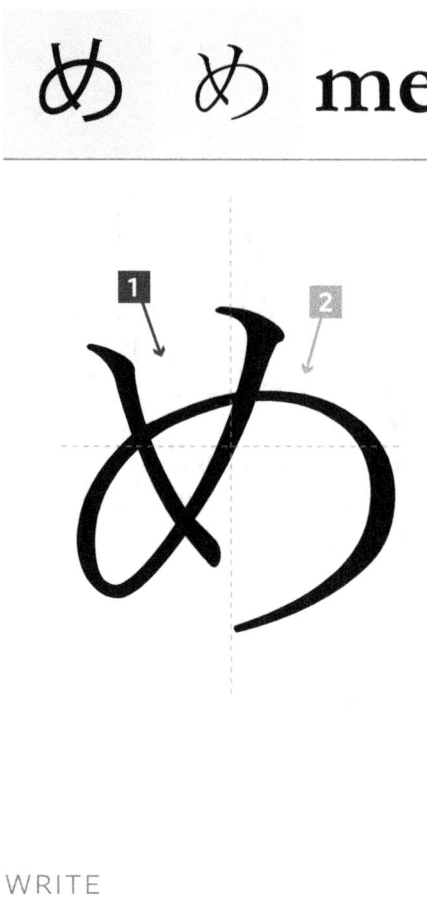

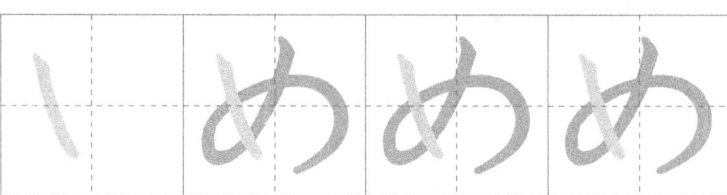

WRITE   First, trace the shapes in the large cells below

PRACTICE   Now practice drawing this character in these smaller cells.

も も **mo**

SPEAK — Pronounced just like the 'mo' in more.

LEARN — This kana has three strokes; long fade, stop, stop.

Just like hiragana し, we start by drawing the shape of a fishing hook and ending with a flick of the pen as it curves around. Your second and third strokes are two parallel, horizontal lines that cut across the first stroke. This can also be seen with the second and third strokes connected in some fonts, shown in the smaller image on the left.

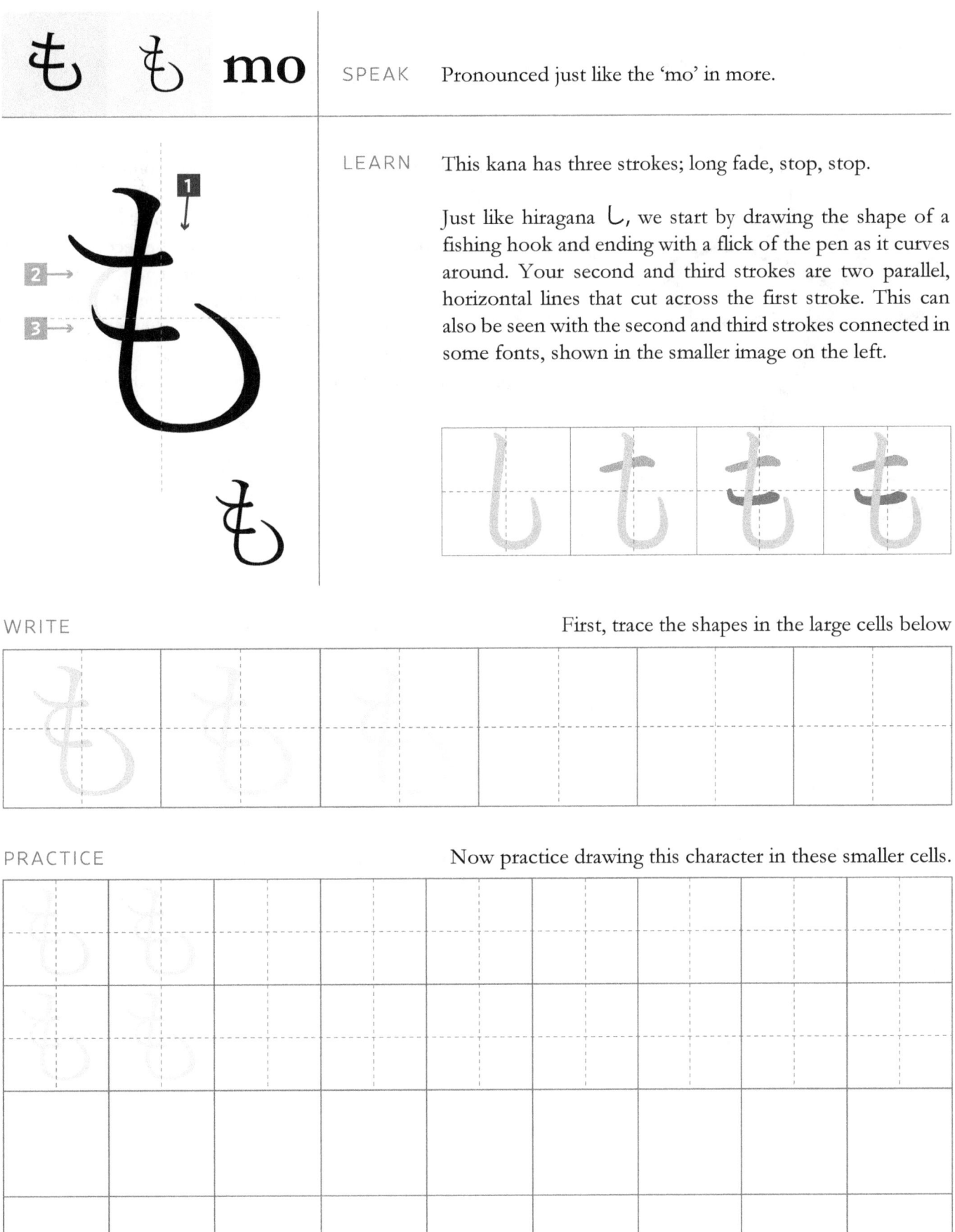

WRITE — First, trace the shapes in the large cells below

PRACTICE — Now practice drawing this character in these smaller cells.

49

SPEAK Pronounced like the 'ya' in yard'

LEARN Draw this kana with three strokes; fade, jump, stop.

Your first stroke starts as a shallow diagonal line up and to the right, before curving back around. The second stroke is a short line at the top near the center. The third and final mark is a longer diagonal line from upper left to lower right - it should intersect with the first stroke about a third of the way across from the left. Also seen with strokes 2 and 3 connected, shown in the smaller image to the left.

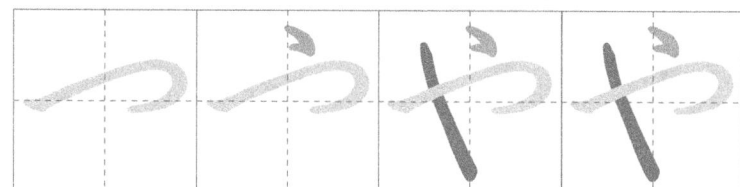

WRITE   First, trace the shapes in the large cells below

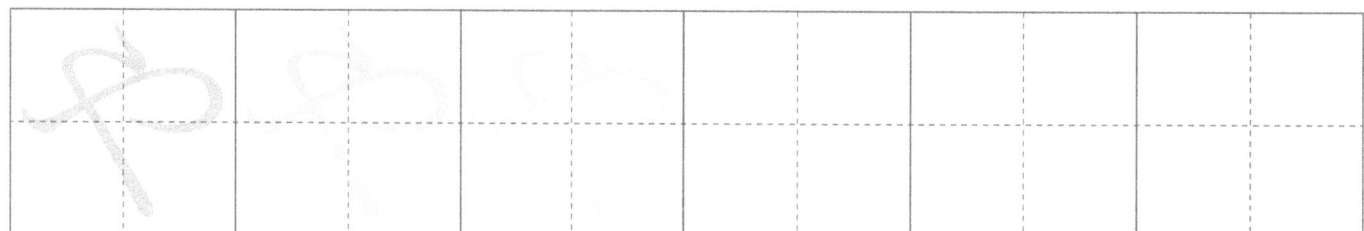

PRACTICE   Now practice drawing this character in these smaller cells.

SPEAK | Pronounced like the 'u' in universal.

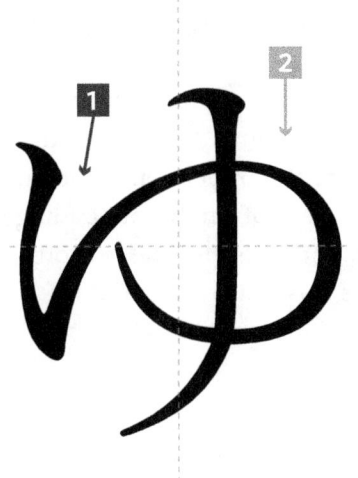

LEARN | This kana is drawn with two strokes; fade, fade.

Begin with a slightly curved line downwards before moving back up a little. Without taking your pen from the page, continue by drawing a large curve that almost closes as a circle on itself. Your second stroke is a vertical line that curves down to the left, cutting through the large curve of the first. Finish the stroke by flicking your pen from the paper to fade it out.

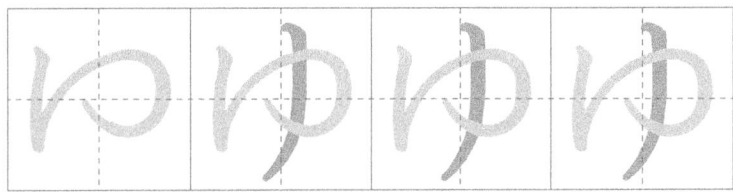

WRITE | First, trace the shapes in the large cells below

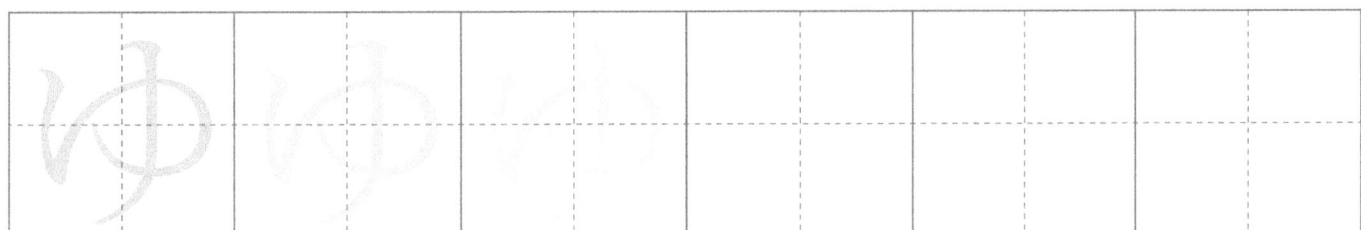

PRACTICE | Now practice drawing this character in these smaller cells.

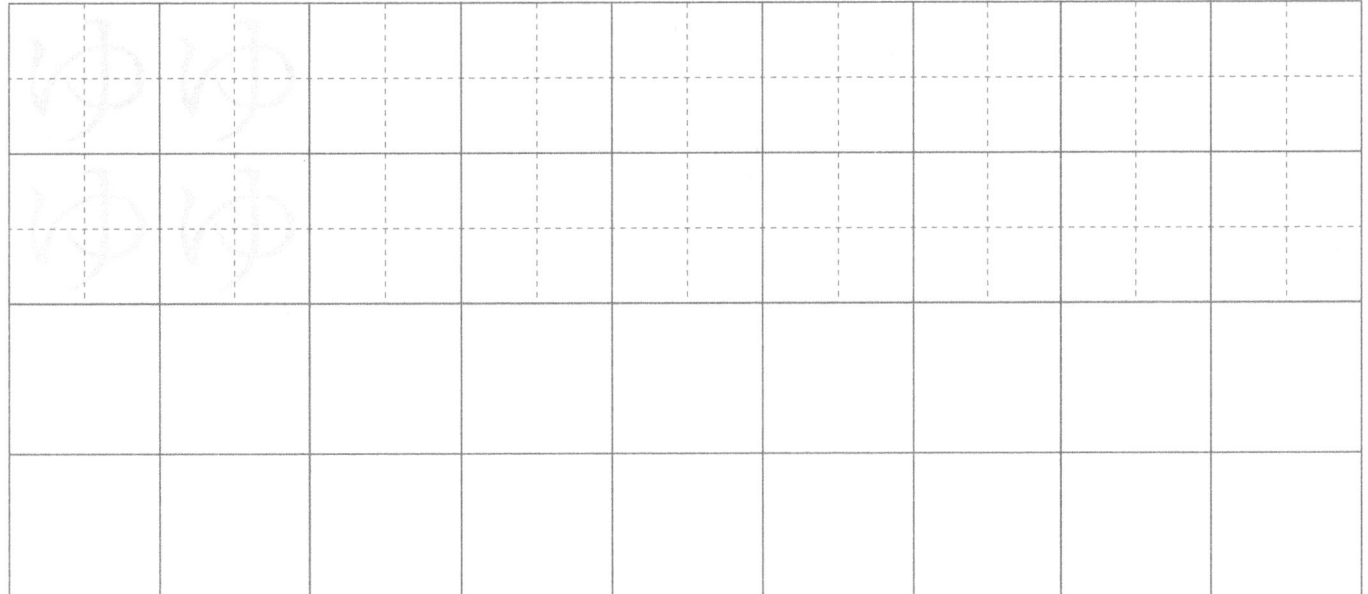

よ　よ　yo

SPEAK Pronounced just like the 'yo' in yo-yo.

LEARN This kana is drawn with two strokes; jump fade, stop.

The first mark is a short horizontal line, starting at the center and moving out to the right. Your second stroke begins as a vertical line from the upper center of the cell, and is drawn down towards the bottom before ending with a small loop over itself and stopping in the bottom right. Don't flick the pen here, as this is a stop mark.

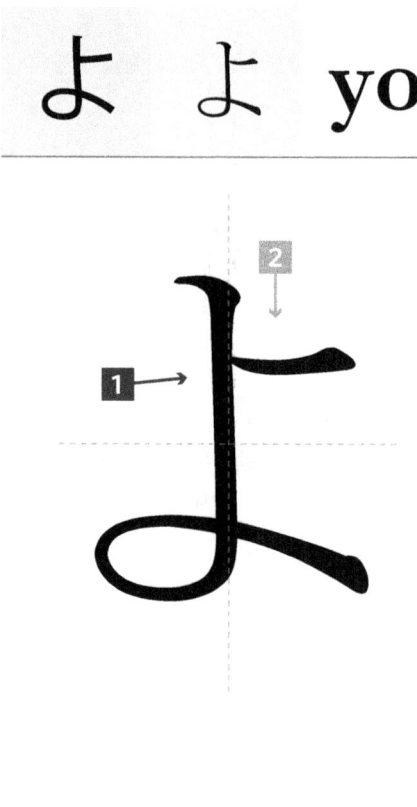

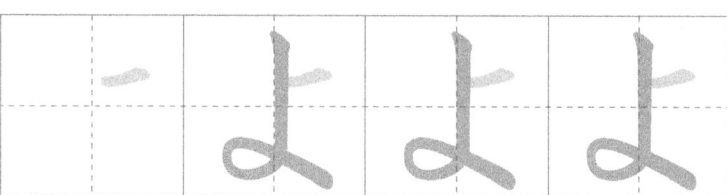

WRITE First, trace the shapes in the large cells below

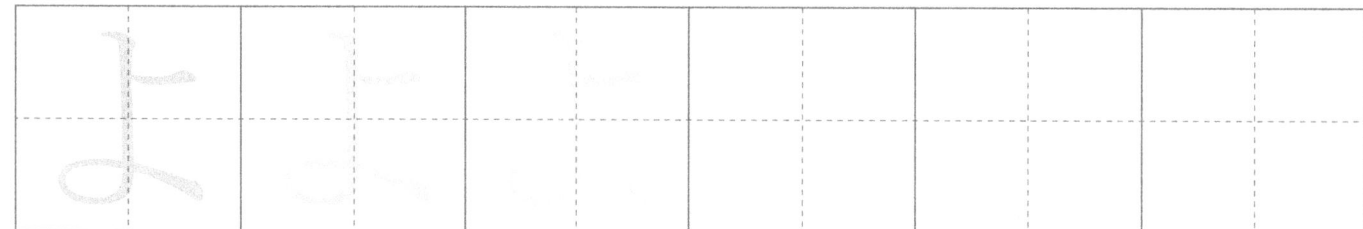

PRACTICE Now practice drawing this character in these smaller cells.

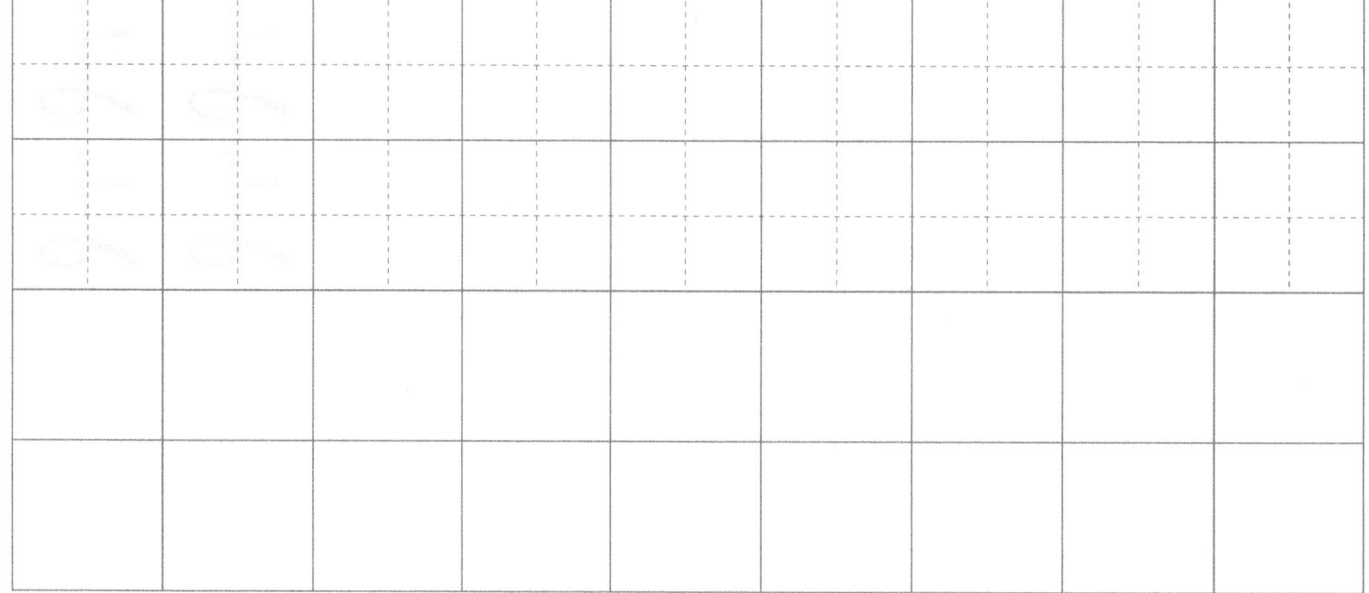

ら ら ra

SPEAK — Pronounced like the 'ra' in ramen.

LEARN — This kana is drawn with two strokes; jump, and a long fade.

The first stroke is a relatively short line, made at an angle near the top of the cell. Then, in a similar way to drawing the number 5, the next mark moves vertically down and then out to the right in a large curve. The curve should move up a little, before turning to come back around and down. End with a flick of your pen. This character can also be seen as a single joined up shape.

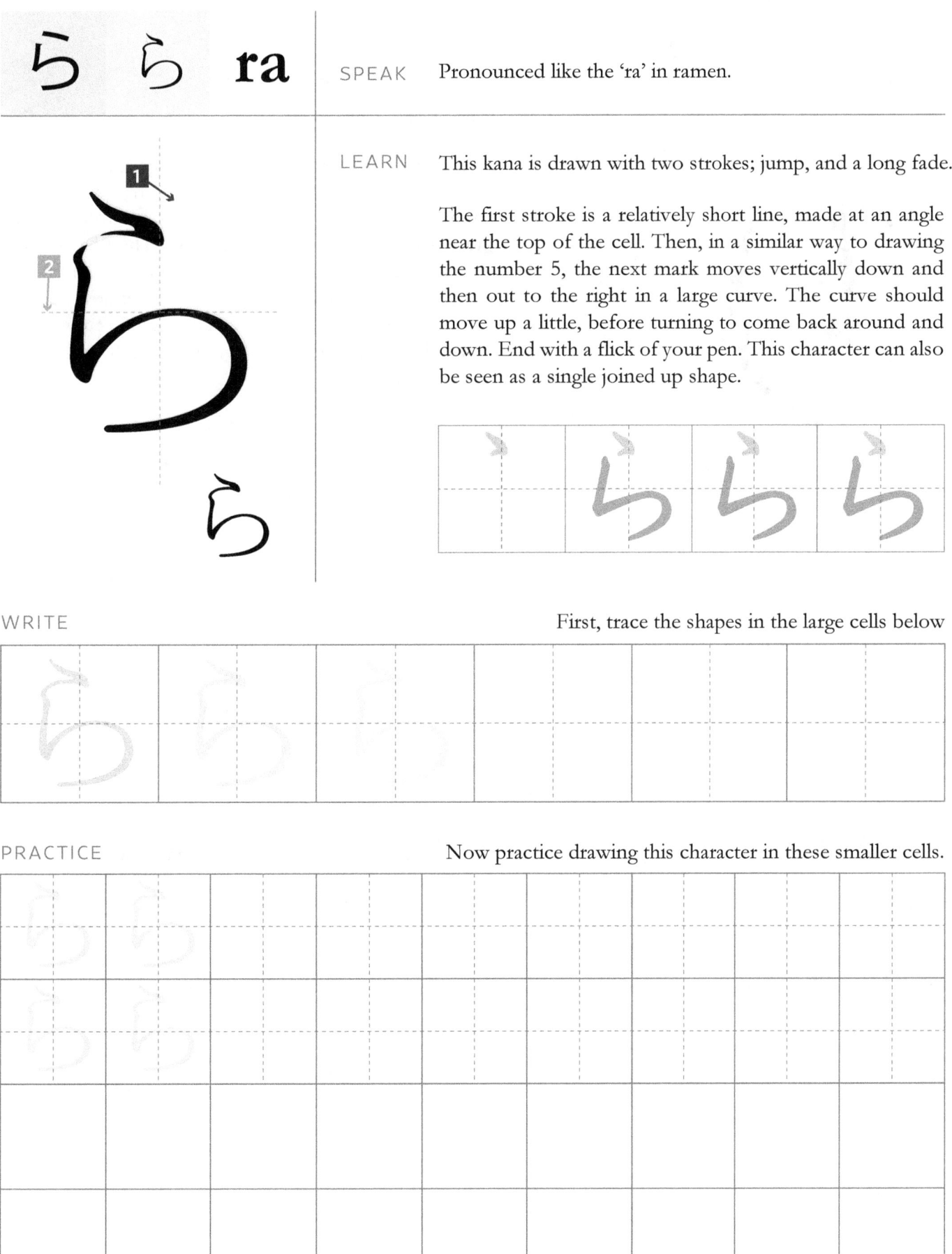

WRITE — First, trace the shapes in the large cells below

PRACTICE — Now practice drawing this character in these smaller cells.

53

り　り　ri

SPEAK — Pronounced like the 'ree' in reef.

LEARN — This kana is drawn with two strokes; jump, fade.

Commonly shown as a single mark, the correct way to write this character is with two strokes. The first is a line going down and finishing with a hane upwards and to the right. As your hane ends, put your pen back down on the paper to create the second stroke. Draw a long curving line down and to the left, flicking your pen from the page at the end to fade it out.

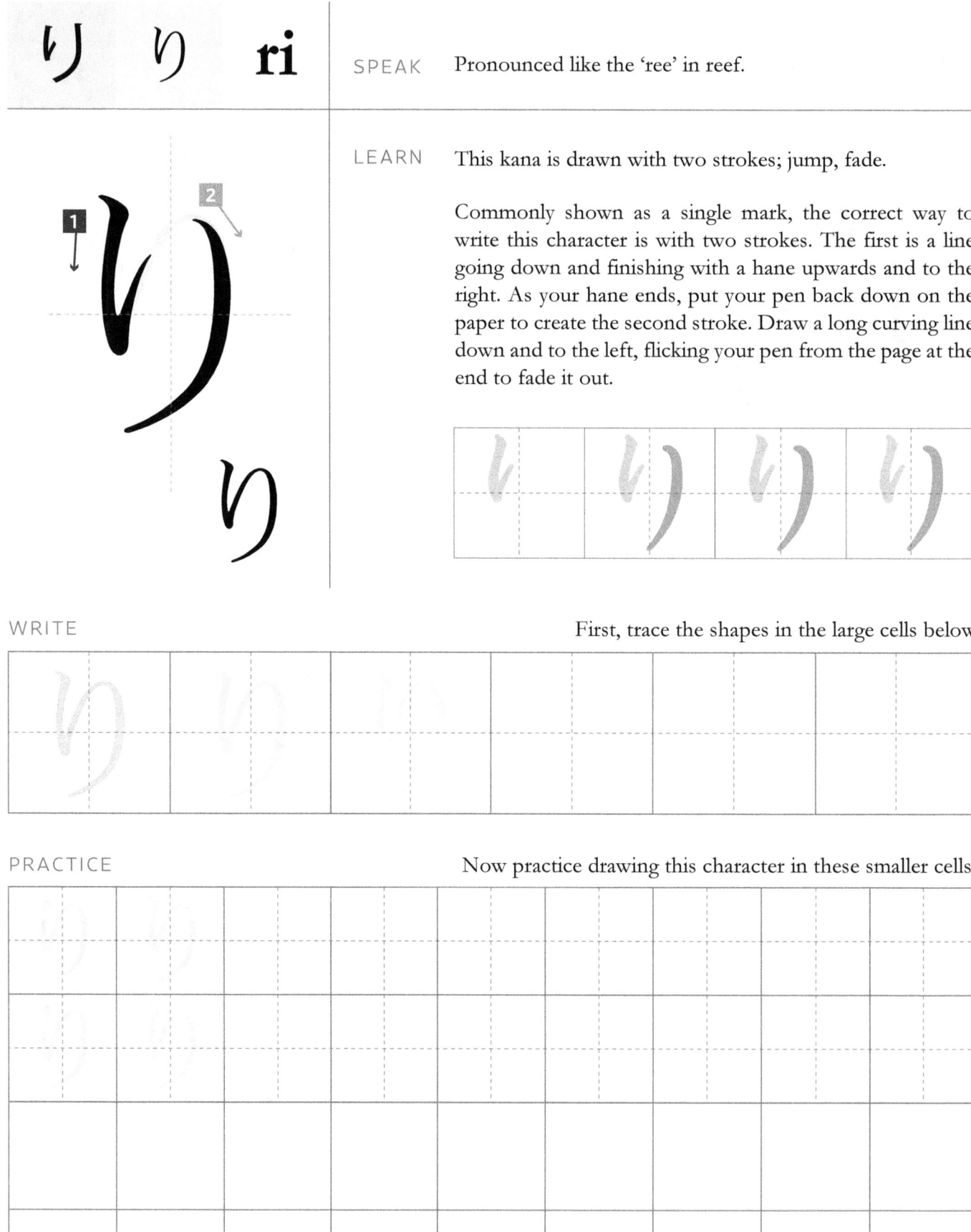

WRITE — First, trace the shapes in the large cells below

PRACTICE — Now practice drawing this character in these smaller cells.

る る **ru**

SPEAK — Pronounced like the 'rew' in brew.

LEARN — This is drawn with one stroke; a long curved zig-zag stop.

This single stroke character begins with a small horizontal line from left to right, before turning and moving down to the left with a longer mark. Without lifting your pen, retrace back up a little and then create a large circular loop, with another, much smaller loop at the end. The smallest loop should not run over or beyond your line, but instead finish on top of it.

WRITE — First, trace the shapes in the large cells below

PRACTICE — Now practice drawing this character in these smaller cells.

れ　れ　re

SPEAK — Pronounced like the 're' in rent.

LEARN — Drawn with two strokes; a stop, then a zig-zag fade

Starting with a vertical line from top to bottom, this kana is made with only two strokes. The second begins with a fairly short horizontal line across the first, before going diagonally down and left, crossing the vertical line once more. Without lifting the pen, retrace back upwards then draw a tall wave shape to the right. At the top, drawn down and curve out and up to the right, ending with a flick.

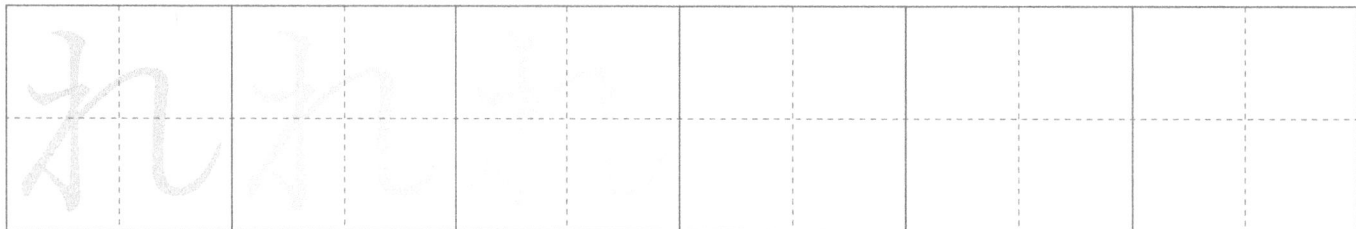

WRITE — First, trace the shapes in the large cells below

PRACTICE — Now practice drawing this character in these smaller cells.

ろ ろ ro

SPEAK — Pronounced like the 'ro' in road.

LEARN — This kana is drawn with one stroke; zig-zag fade.

We write the ろ in much the same way as writing る, except without a loop at the end. Start with a fairly short horizontal short line from left to right, and follow with a diagonal line down and back to the left. Trace back upwards a little and then finish the stroke off by making the large curve out to the right and back in - all in one smooth action, ending with a flick from the page.

WRITE — First, trace the shapes in the large cells below

PRACTICE — Now practice drawing this character in these smaller cells.

わ わ **wa**

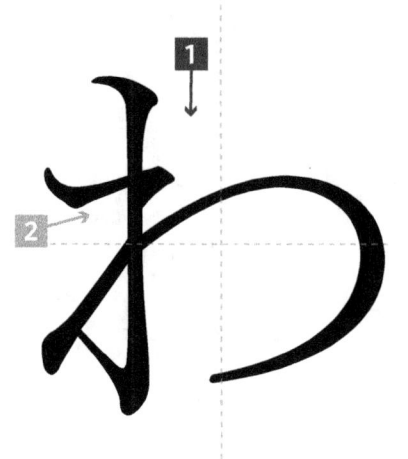

SPEAK   Pronounced like the 'wa' in wagon.

LEARN   This kana is drawn with two strokes; stop, zig-zag fade.

Begin with the vertical mark from top to bottom, left of the center and ending with a hane up and left. Your second line passes across the first stroke and then moves diagonally down to the left and cutting through the first one again. Complete this stroke by drawing the large curve out to the right and back around, fading it at the end with a flick.

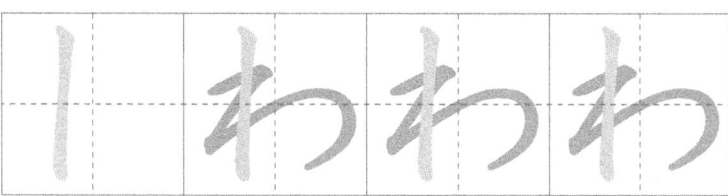

WRITE   First, trace the shapes in the large cells below

PRACTICE   Now practice drawing this character in these smaller cells.

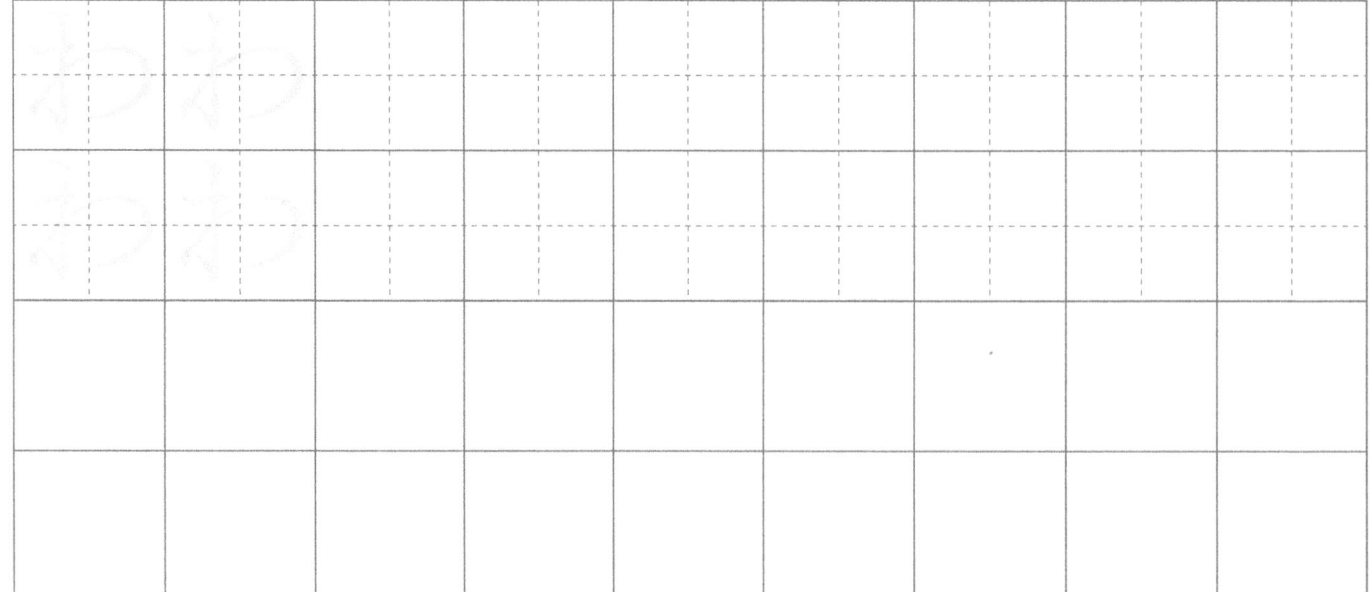

58

を を wo*

SPEAK — Pronounced like the 'oh' in woah, with a silent 'w'.

LEARN — Drawn with three strokes; each of which is a stop.

Your first stroke is a horizontal line from left to right. The second mark begins as a diagonal line crossing the first stroke, before turning up and back down. It should end at a lower point to where your pen turned before. Your third line is a curve that starts from the right side, above the center line, and cuts through the end of the second stroke. It returns to the lower right of the cell, ending with a stop.

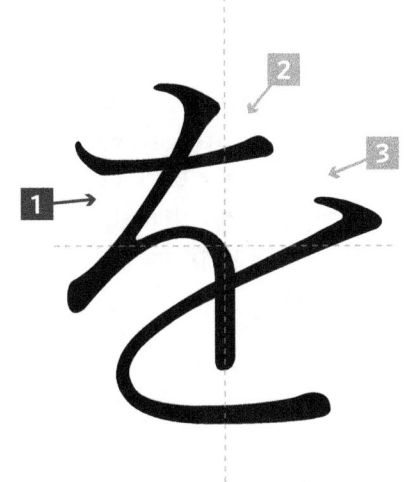

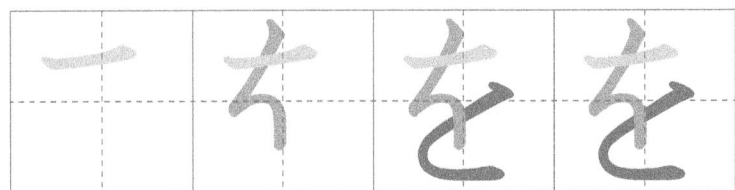

Uncommon kana, used as a particle.

WRITE — First, trace the shapes in the large cells below

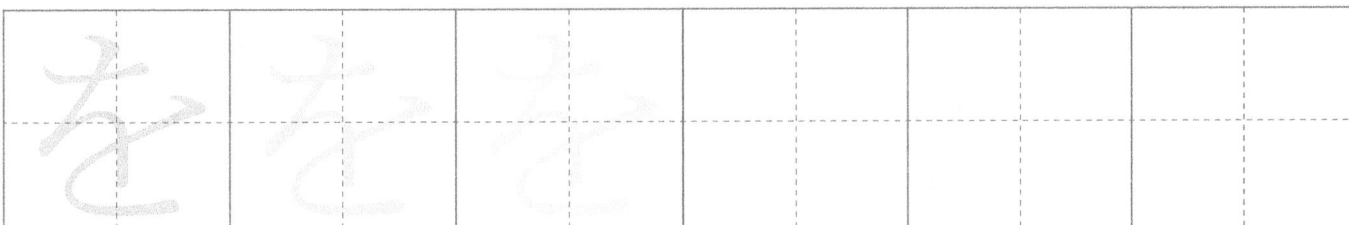

PRACTICE — Now practice drawing this character in these smaller cells.

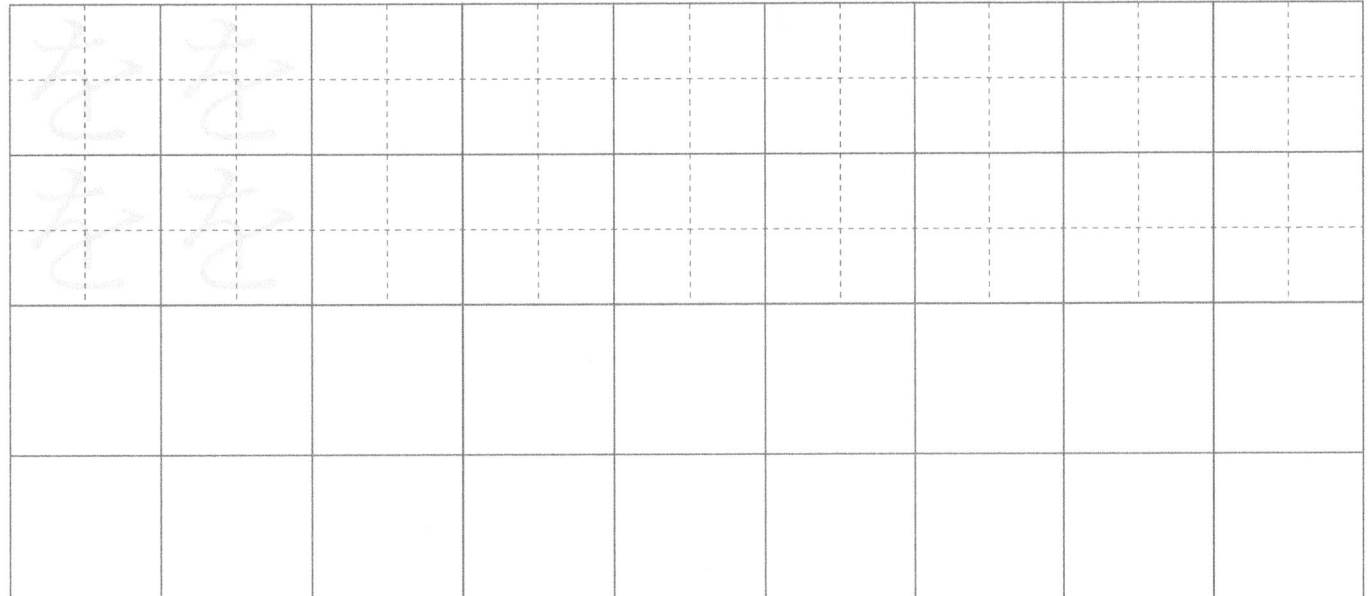

59

ん ん **n**

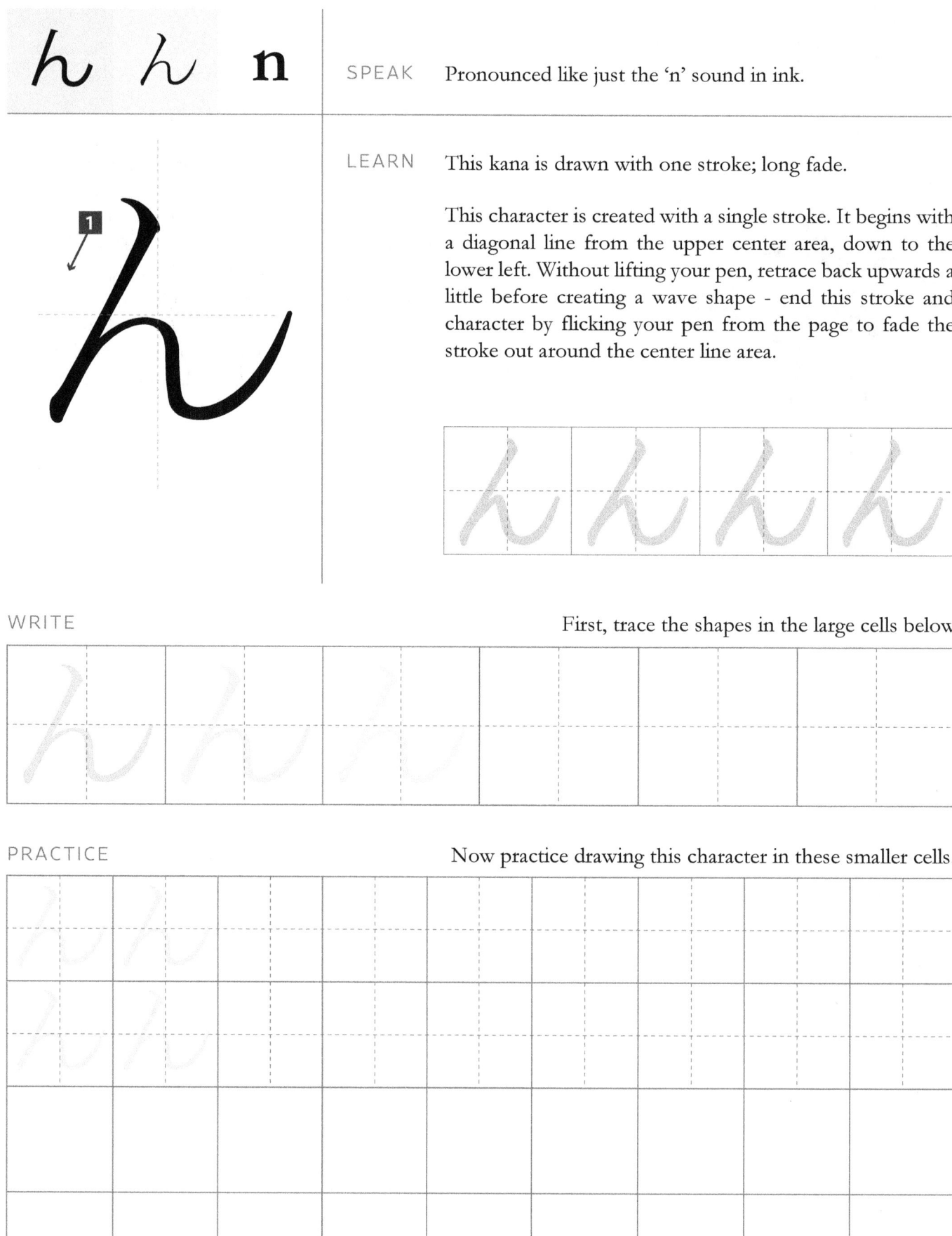

SPEAK — Pronounced like just the 'n' sound in ink.

LEARN — This kana is drawn with one stroke; long fade.

This character is created with a single stroke. It begins with a diagonal line from the upper center area, down to the lower left. Without lifting your pen, retrace back upwards a little before creating a wave shape - end this stroke and character by flicking your pen from the page to fade the stroke out around the center line area.

WRITE — First, trace the shapes in the large cells below

PRACTICE — Now practice drawing this character in these smaller cells.

Part 4
KATAKANA CHARTS & BASIC RULES

Katakana Chart

This chart shows the 46 basic Katakana with a *spelling* in Romaji for a similar phonetic sound. The vowel sounds are at the top and their counterpart versions with consonant sounds are shown below them. **note the exception 'n' - also, *wo is an uncommon kana.*

Vowel Sounds

	a	i	u	e	o
	ア a	イ i	ウ u	エ e	オ o
k	カ ka	キ ki	ク ku	ケ ke	コ ko
s	サ sa	シ shi	ス su	セ se	ソ so
t	タ ta	チ chi	ツ tsu	テ te	ト to
n	ナ na	ニ ni	ヌ nu	ネ ne	ノ no
h	ハ ha	ヒ hi	フ fu	ヘ he	ホ ho
m	マ ma	ミ mi	ム mu	メ me	モ mo
y	ヤ ya		ユ yu		ヨ yo
r	ラ ra	リ ri	ル ru	レ re	ロ ro
w	ワ wa		ン **n		ヲ *wo

Consonants

Modifiers

DIACRITICS

Just as with *Hiragana*, there are **25 Diacritic** symbols in **Katakana**. They are used in the same way, to show when similar sounding syllables need to be voiced differently. Even more conveniently, the marks to show this change in sound are identical:

ホ ho — Basic   ボ bo — *with Dakuten*   ポ po — *with Handakuten*

The rules for Katakana diacritic symbols work the same way. *Dakuten* and *Handakuten* show us that the consonant part of the sound needs to be changed when spoken:

- **k**-sound are pronounced with a **g**-sound.
- **s**-sounds change to a **z**-sound *(except for し)*.
- **t**-sounds become **d**-sounds.
- **h**-sounds become **b**-sounds with *Dakuten*.
  ...or **P**-sounds with the *Handakuten*.

	a	i	u	e	o
k ▶ g	ガ ga	ギ gi	グ gu	ゲ ge	ゴ go
s ▶ z	ザ za	ジ ji	ズ zu	ゼ ze	ゾ zo
t ▶ d	ダ da	ヂ dzi (ji)	ヅ dzu	デ de	ド do
h ▶ b	バ ba	ビ bi	ブ bu	ベ be	ボ bo
h ▶ p	パ pa	ピ pi	プ pu	ペ pe	ポ po

DIGRAPHS

Here are the **Digraphs** for Katakana too - once more, we use two basic characters to show where two syllable sounds are combined to make another one. *Easy, right?*

キ + ヤ = キャ
(ki)   (ya)   (kya)

The characters used have the same sounds as the two corresponding Hiragana. The importance of writing the second symbol smaller than the first still applies.

Pronunciation of these so-called *compound Katakana* sounds is just as simple - for example, キ (ki) + ヤ (ya) becomes キャ (kya) and we pronounce it as 'kiya' *without the 'i' sound.*

This table looks complex but just remember that Digraphs are made *exclusively* with letters from the イ/i column *(excluding itself)* **and** modified by letters from row **Y**!

キャ kya	キュ kyu	キョ kyo	ギャ gya	ギュ gyu	ギョ gyo
シャ sha	シュ shu	ショ sho	ジャ ja	ジュ ju	ジョ jo
チャ cha	チュ chu	チョ cho	ニャ nya	ニュ nyu	ニョ nyo
ニャ hya	ヒュ hyu	ヒョ hyo	ビャ bya	ビュ byu	ビョ byo
ピャ pya	ピュ pyu	ピョ pyo	リャ rya	リュ ryu	リョ ryo
ミャ mya	ミュ myu	ミョ myo			

Modifiers

Modifiers

DOUBLE CONSONANTS

Japanese words with Katakana can contain a *double consonant sound* too. These words also feature the small ツ / **tsu** *(called sokuon)* to show that it should be pronounced differently. Let's look at another example for Katakana:

ペット
(pe ッ ← to)   petto

Without the small ツ *(tsu)*, the word ペト *(peto)* doesn't have any meaning but ペット *(petto)*, with the *sokuon*, means **pet** - like a hamster or cat!

Notice that the small ツ is placed **before** the character that it takes the extra consonant sound from. When you see words with this modifier, the consonant part of the symbol that follows it *(in this example, the 't' from 'to')* is added to the end of the sound before it.

Both consonants need to be heard separately when the word is spoken, like saying **'pet-to'** but without leaving a gap than can be heard.

LONG VOWEL SOUNDS

We still need to be aware of elongated vowel sounds *(e.g. aa, ii. oo, ee, and uu)*. When spoken, the duration of the sound is extended (usually double again) but when written in Katakana we use a line ー *(called* 伸ばし棒*, which literally means 'stretching bar')*.

This is one way Katakana differs from Hiragana, aside from the shapes, as that uses an additional vowel symbol to denote a long vowel sound. Let's look at some examples:

フ + リ = フリー   ケ + キ = ケーキ
(fu) (ri)—   fu-rii *(free)*   (ke)— (ki)   kee-ki *(cake)*

It is worth noting that the 'stretching bar' is rotated to a vertical line when text is written vertically.

Part 5

LEARN HOW TO WRITE KATAKANA

ア ア	a

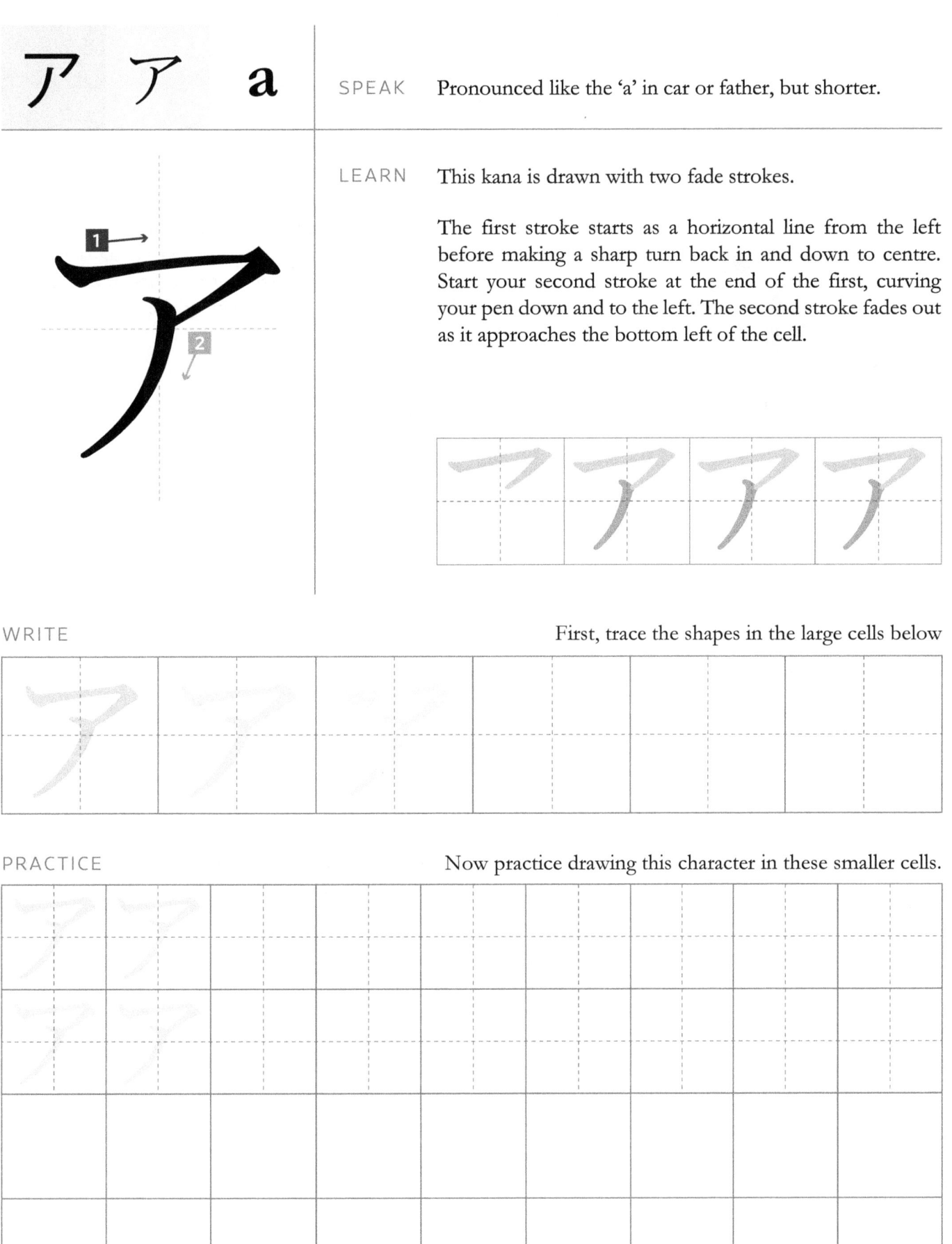

SPEAK — Pronounced like the 'a' in car or father, but shorter.

LEARN — This kana is drawn with two fade strokes.

The first stroke starts as a horizontal line from the left before making a sharp turn back in and down to centre. Start your second stroke at the end of the first, curving your pen down and to the left. The second stroke fades out as it approaches the bottom left of the cell.

WRITE — First, trace the shapes in the large cells below

PRACTICE — Now practice drawing this character in these smaller cells.

イ イ i

SPEAK　Pronounced like the 'ee' in eel.

LEARN　This kana is drawn with two strokes; a fade and a stop.

Your first mark is a slightly curved diagonal line, beginning high in the upper right of the cell, and fading out in the bottom left. The next stroke starts around the centre of your first stroke, just to the right of the middle, moving straight down to a stop near the bottom.

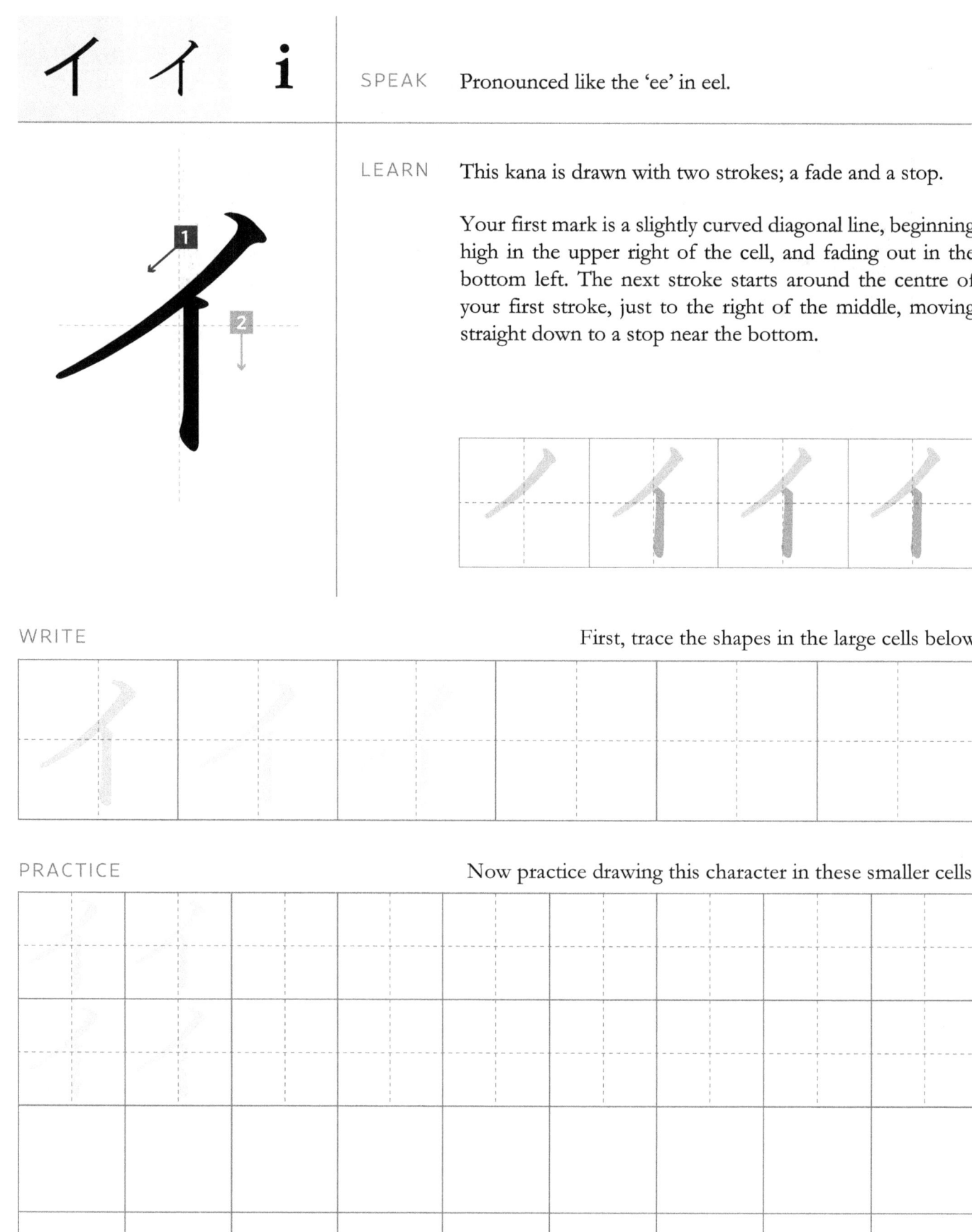

WRITE　First, trace the shapes in the large cells below

PRACTICE　Now practice drawing this character in these smaller cells.

ウ ウ u

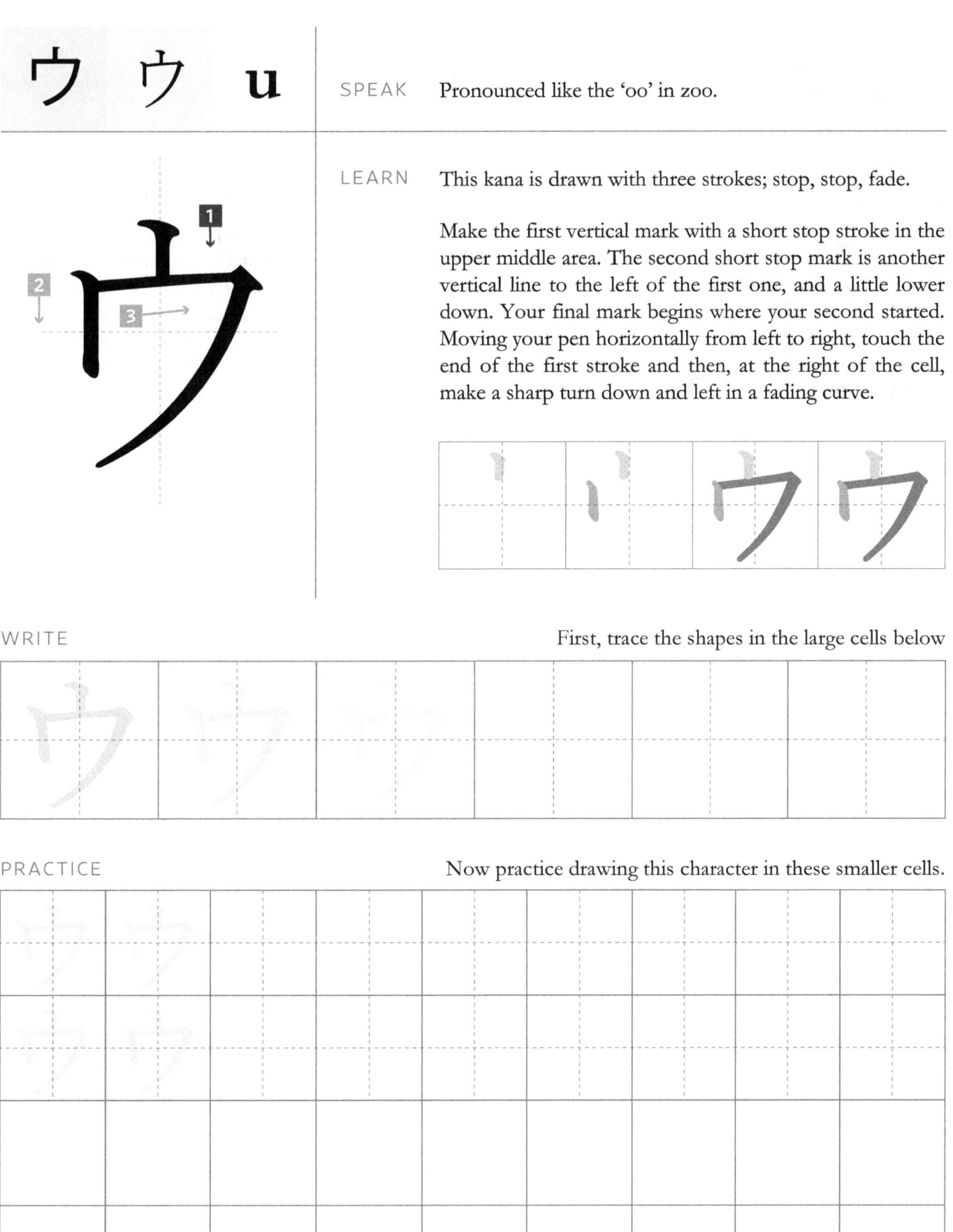

SPEAK — Pronounced like the 'oo' in zoo.

LEARN — This kana is drawn with three strokes; stop, stop, fade.

Make the first vertical mark with a short stop stroke in the upper middle area. The second short stop mark is another vertical line to the left of the first one, and a little lower down. Your final mark begins where your second started. Moving your pen horizontally from left to right, touch the end of the first stroke and then, at the right of the cell, make a sharp turn down and left in a fading curve.

WRITE — First, trace the shapes in the large cells below

PRACTICE — Now practice drawing this character in these smaller cells.

エ　エ　e

SPEAK — Pronounced as 'eh' like the 'e' in men.

LEARN — This kana is drawn with three strokes; all stops.

Start with the horizontal line across the middle in the upper part of the cell. Your second mark then starts in the middle of the first, drawn down the center line. The final stroke is another horizontal line, from left to right, that passes across the end of the second mark at the center. To make sure your writing has good balance, your final mark should be wider than the first one.

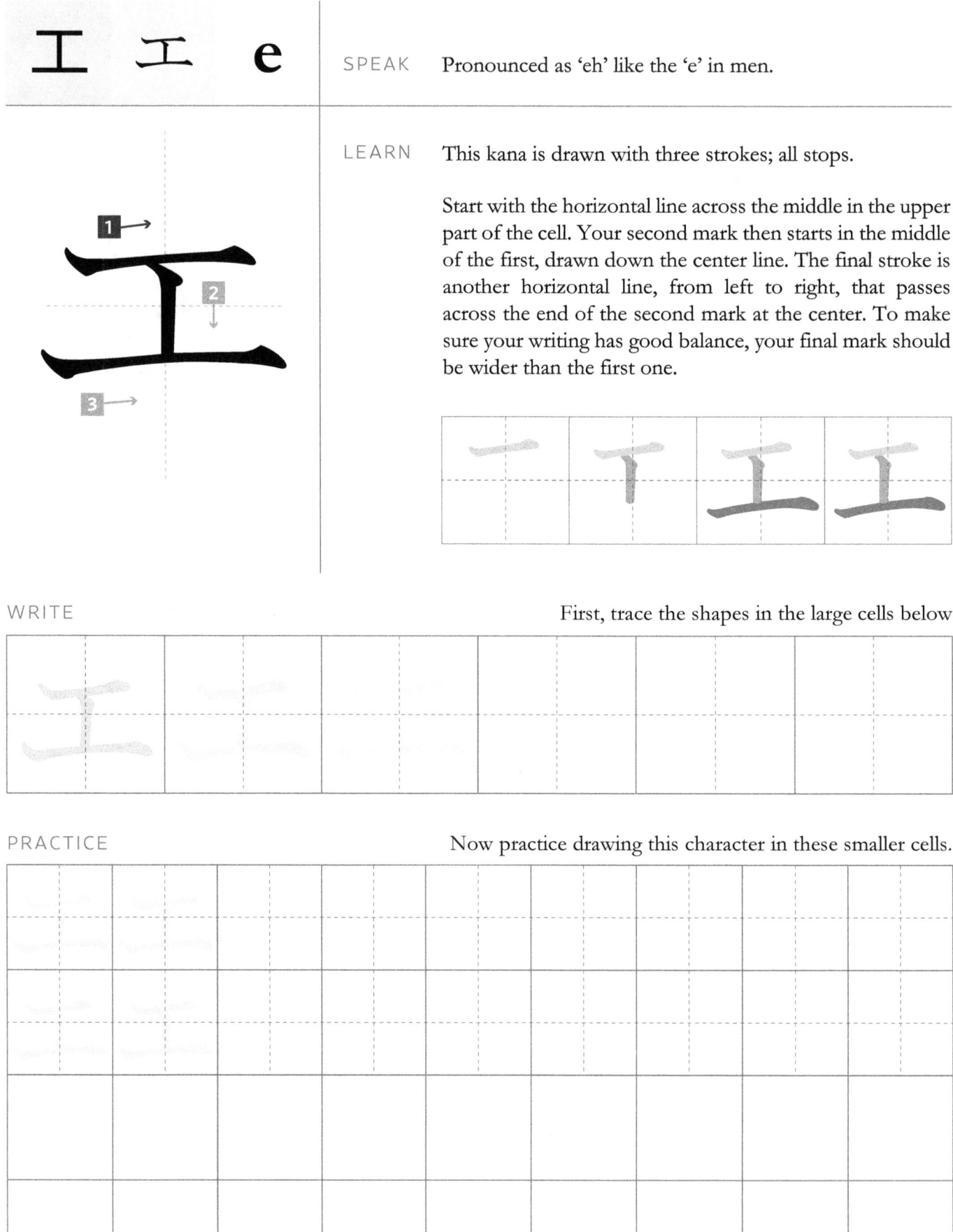

WRITE — First, trace the shapes in the large cells below

PRACTICE — Now practice drawing this character in these smaller cells.

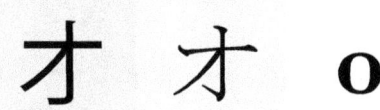

SPEAK   Pronounced like the 'o' in original.

LEARN   This kana has three strokes; stop, jump fade, and fade.

Start by drawing a long horizontal line from left to right. Your second stroke is a vertical line that intersects with the first around one third of the way from the right side. Finish the second stroke by flicking your pen from the page (this is called a hane). Your final stroke starts at the intersection of strokes 1 and 2, and curves down and left with a fade - it should not extend lower than the second stroke.

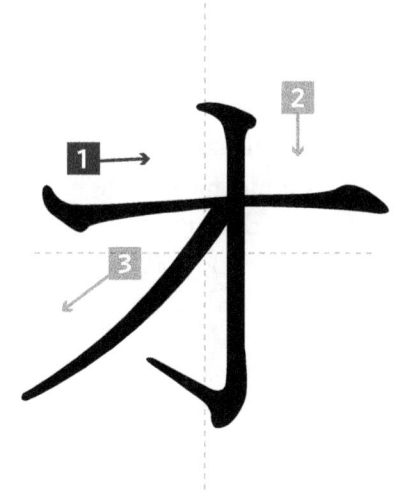

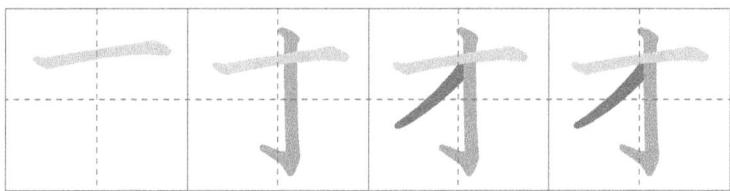

WRITE   First, trace the shapes in the large cells below

PRACTICE   Now practice drawing this character in these smaller cells.

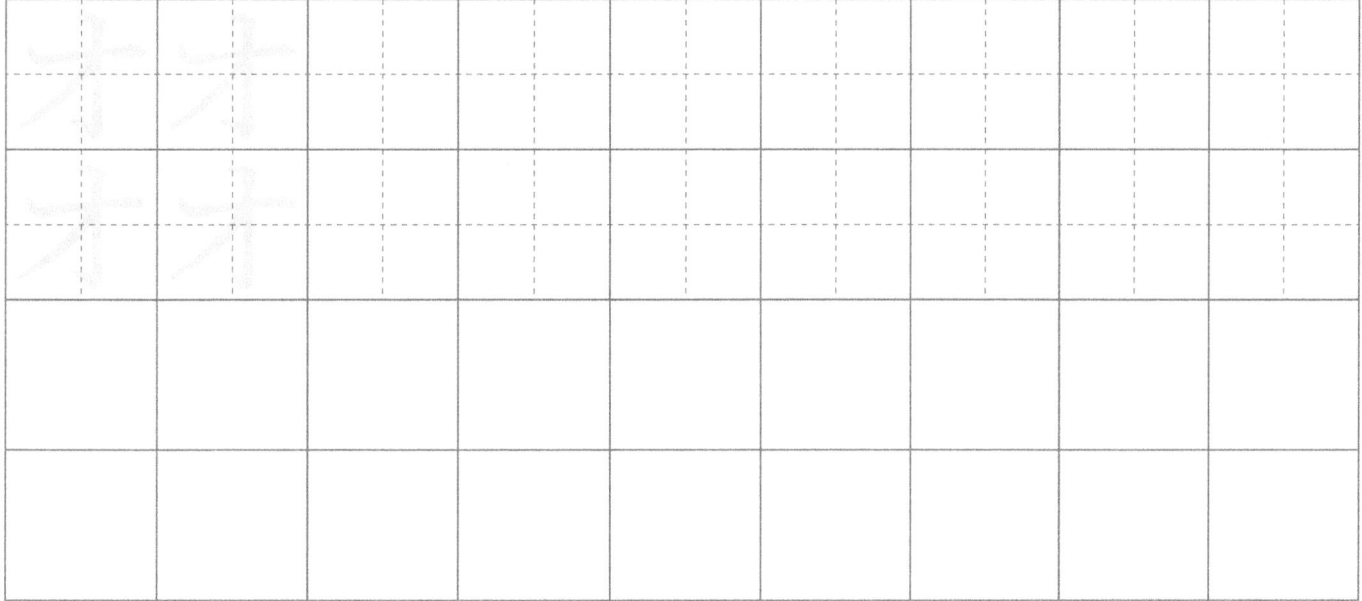

71

カ カ ka

SPEAK — Pronounced like 'car' but without the 'r' sound.

LEARN — This kana is drawn with two strokes; jump fade, stop.

This is an angular version of hiragana か and starts with a slightly inclined horizontal line that turns downwards sharply. The downwards part should have a slight curve backwards and diagonally left. End this stroke with a hane by flicking your pen from the paper. Your second stroke is diagonal line down, with a curve to the left and up.

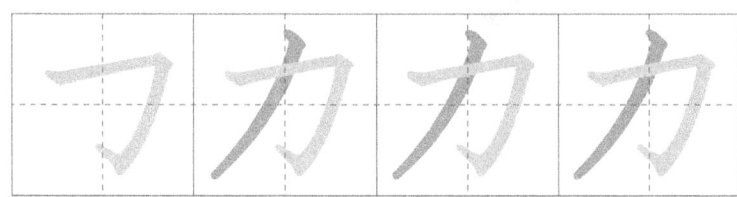

WRITE — First, trace the shapes in the large cells below

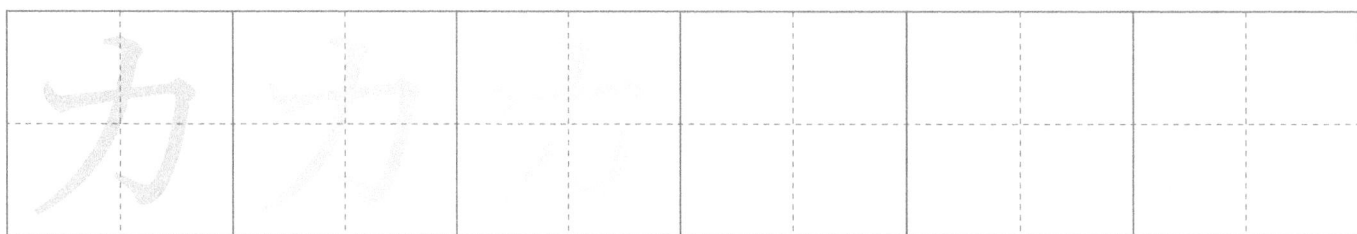

PRACTICE — Now practice drawing this character in these smaller cells.

SPEAK	Pronounced like 'key'.

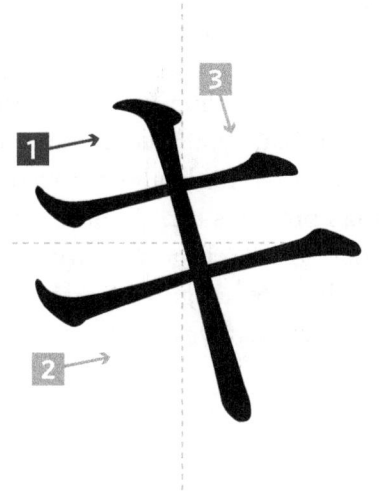

LEARN	Drawn with three strokes; stop, stop, and stop.
	You will notice that this Katakana is also very similar to the Hiragana counterpart - strokes 1 and 2 are parallel diagonal lines from left to right, in an upwards direction, the second slightly longer than the first. Your final mark is simply another straight diagonal line, from upper left to lower right. It should cut roughly through the middles of your first two strokes.

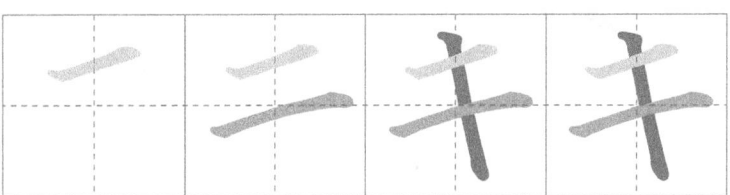

WRITE   First, trace the shapes in the large cells below

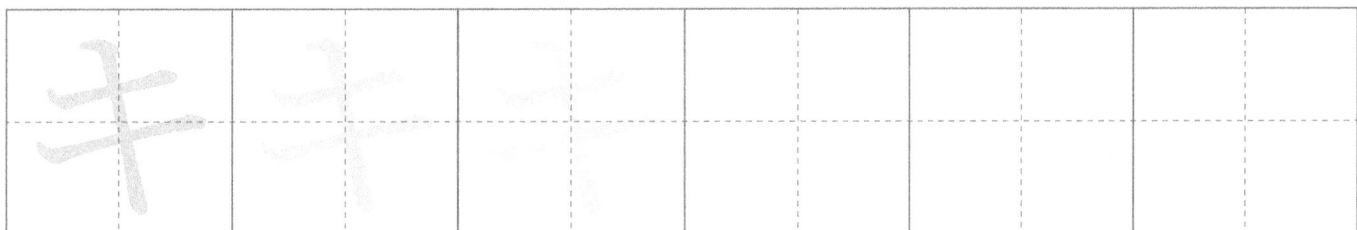

PRACTICE   Now practice drawing this character in these smaller cells.

ク ク **ku**

SPEAK — Pronounced like the 'koo' in cuckoo.

LEARN — This kana is drawn with two strokes; both fades.

Start with the first curved diagonal line from the upper middle, down and to the left. Start your second stroke in roughly the same place as your first. It's begins with a much shorter horizontal mark than previous kana, before a sharp turn and into another much longer diagonal curve down and left. Practice making the two diagonal parts run in parallel to one another for extra neat writing!

WRITE — First, trace the shapes in the large cells below

PRACTICE — Now practice drawing this character in these smaller cells.

ケ ケ **ke**

SPEAK — Pronounced like the 'ke' in Kenneth

LEARN — This kana has three strokes: fade, stop, fade.

Starting in a similar way to the previous katakana ク, draw the first diagonal line and end with a fade by reducing the pressure and gently lifting your pen. The second mark starts from the middle of your first line this time, and is just a longer horizontal line that stops. Begin the third stroke at the midpoint of the second line, and move your pen in a curve down and to the left with a fade - parallel to the first.

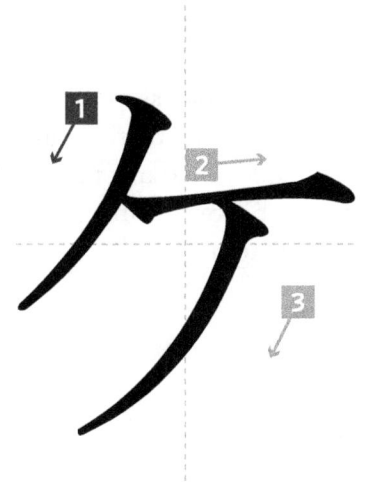

WRITE — First, trace the shapes in the large cells below

PRACTICE — Now practice drawing this character in these smaller cells.

75

コ　コ　ko

SPEAK — Pronounced like the 'co' in core

LEARN — This kana is drawn with two strokes: both stops.

The first mark is a horizontal line that stops and turns downwards quite sharply. Your second mark is another horizontal stroke from the left, and should meet the end of your first stroke with a stop. The two horizontal parts should be parallel and the same length.

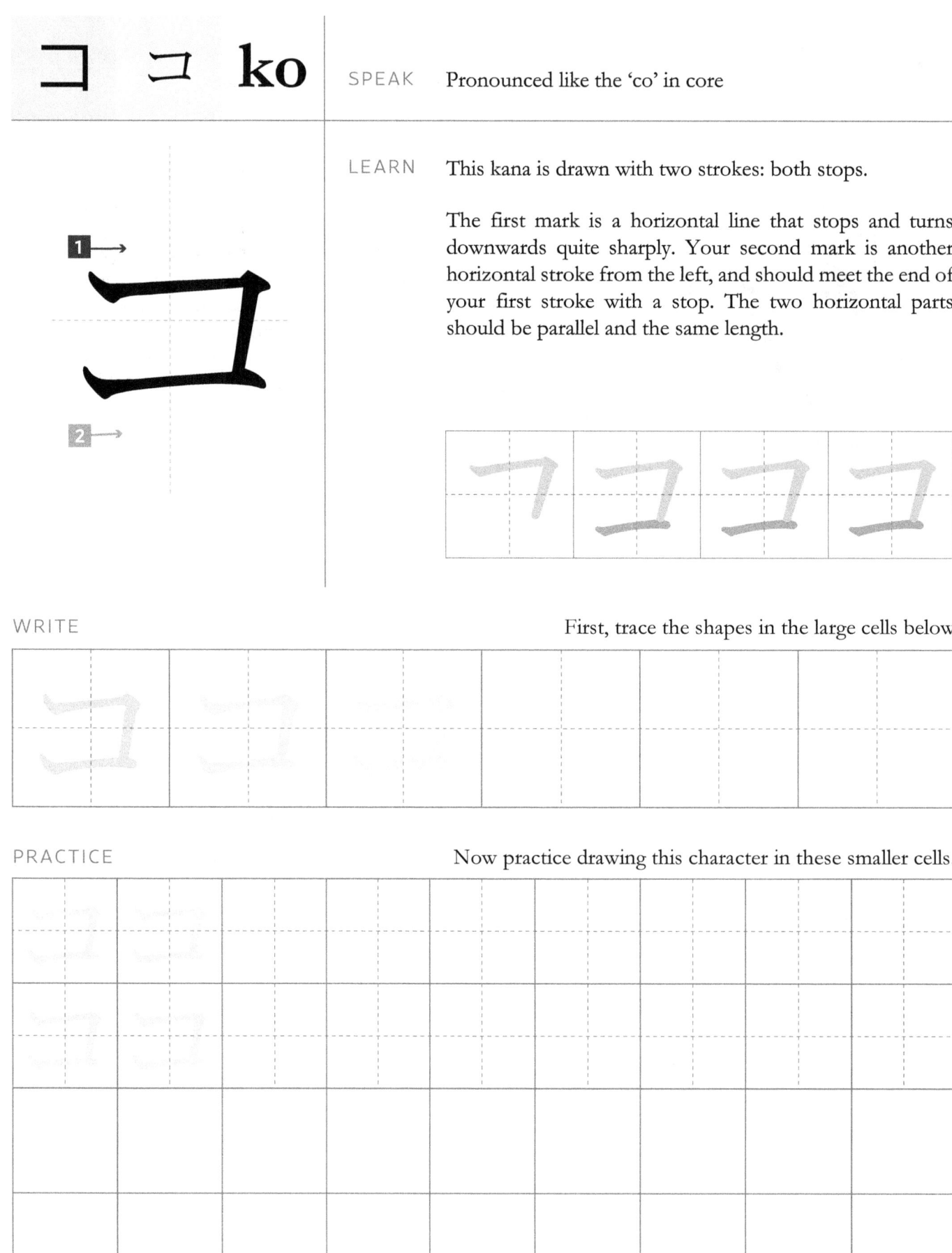

WRITE — First, trace the shapes in the large cells below

PRACTICE — Now practice drawing this character in these smaller cells.

サ サ **sa**

SPEAK | Pronounced like the 'sa' in sardines.

LEARN | This kana is drawn with three strokes: stop, stop, fade.

Start this kana with a long horizontal line. Your second line cuts through the first one roughly one third from the left, drawn straight down to a stop. The third stroke is a longer curved line that cuts through the first, roughly one third of the length across from the right. It starts as a vertical line before the intersection but curves left after crossing down through your first stroke.

WRITE | First, trace the shapes in the large cells below

PRACTICE | Now practice drawing this character in these smaller cells.

77

シ シ shi

SPEAK — Pronounced like 'she' as in sheet.

LEARN — Draw this kana with three strokes; stop, stop, fade.

Both the first and second strokes are short stop marks, made in parallel and at a slight angle down. Your third stroke begins in the lower left area, below the first strokes, and curves up and to the right. You should pay special attention to the spacing of the three strokes and the points that they start from. We will see some very similar looking characters further ahead.

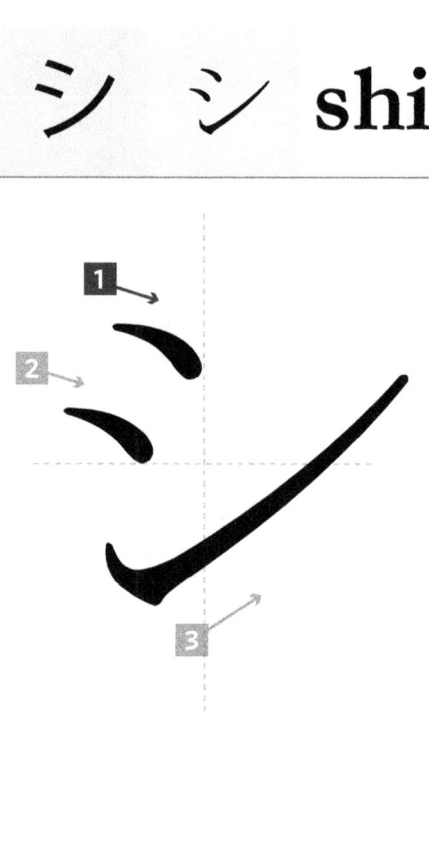

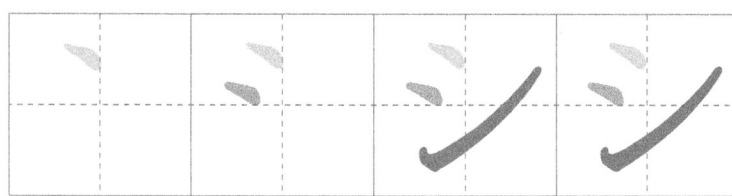

WRITE — First, trace the shapes in the large cells below

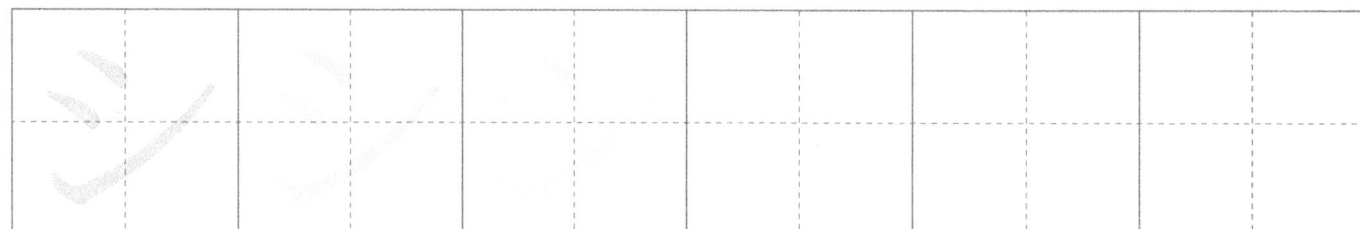

PRACTICE — Now practice drawing this character in these smaller cells.

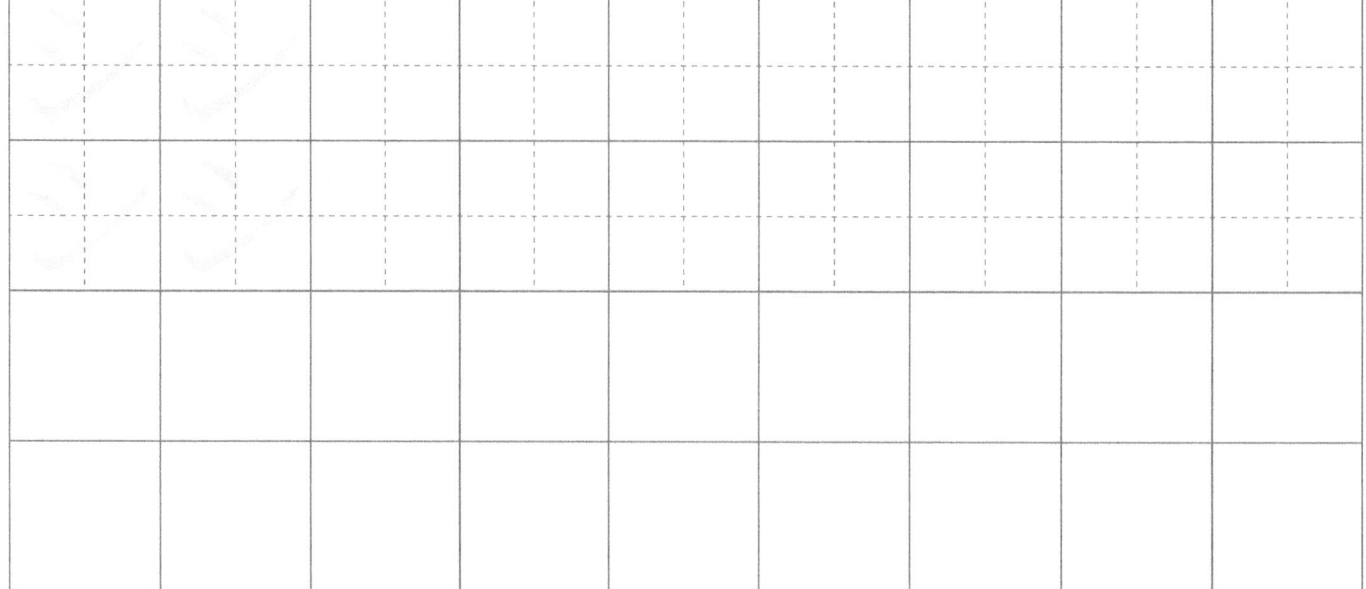

ス　ス　**su**

SPEAK　Pronounced like the 'su' in super

LEARN　This has two strokes; a long fade, and a stop.

This character begins with a stroke that we have made in earlier kana. It starts with a horizontal line from left to right before that sharp turn into a curve, moving down and back to the left in a fade. Your second mark is a relatively short stop stroke, and starts from around the midpoint of your curve from the first stroke.

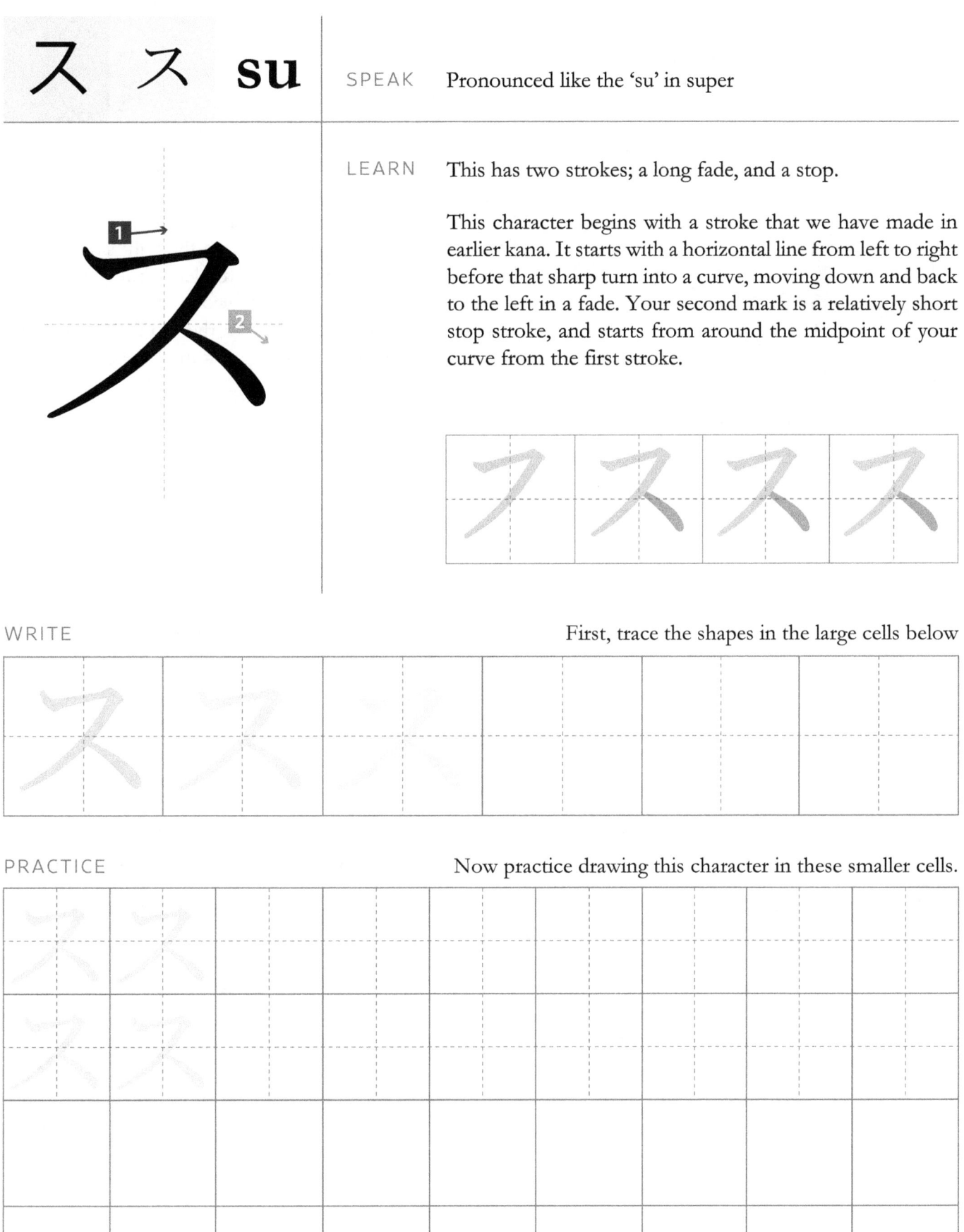

WRITE　First, trace the shapes in the large cells below

PRACTICE　Now practice drawing this character in these smaller cells.

セ　セ　**se**

SPEAK　Pronounced like 'say' but with less 'y'.

LEARN　This kana is drawn with two strokes; a fade and a stop.

Begin the first stroke with a relatively long, inclined line from left to right. As you approach the right side, it turns into a short fade down and to the left - but not quite as sharply as other kana. Your second mark begins as a straight vertical line, drawn from the top and then gently sweeping to the right, near the bottom of the cell.

WRITE　　　　　　　　　　First, trace the shapes in the large cells below

PRACTICE　　　　　　　　Now practice drawing this character in these smaller cells.

ソ ソ **so**

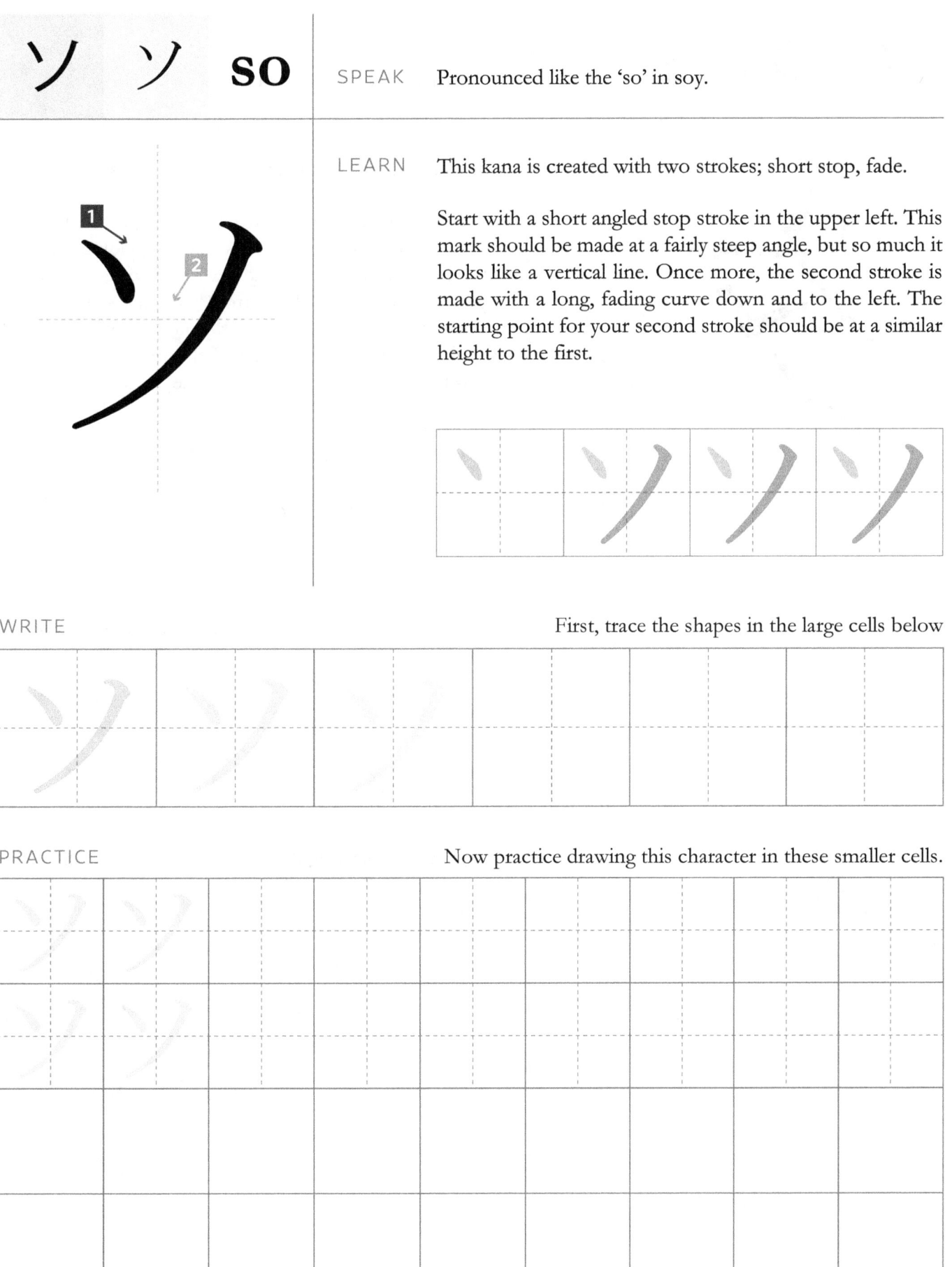

SPEAK — Pronounced like the 'so' in soy.

LEARN — This kana is created with two strokes; short stop, fade.

Start with a short angled stop stroke in the upper left. This mark should be made at a fairly steep angle, but so much it looks like a vertical line. Once more, the second stroke is made with a long, fading curve down and to the left. The starting point for your second stroke should be at a similar height to the first.

WRITE — First, trace the shapes in the large cells below

PRACTICE — Now practice drawing this character in these smaller cells.

81

タ　タ　ta

SPEAK — Pronounced like the 'ta' in target.

LEARN — This kana is drawn with three strokes; fade, fade, stop.

Another kana with some now familiar shapes. In a similar way to ク and ケ, your first stroke is a fading diagonal curve from upper center to lower left. The second stroke begins with a horizontal line from the same start point as the first, curving down to the left. Your last mark is a short diagonal line from the middle of the first stroke. It cuts across the middle of the second stroke.

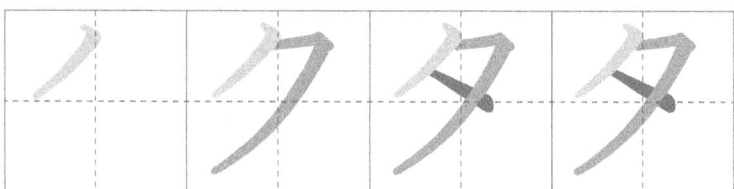

WRITE — First, trace the shapes in the large cells below

PRACTICE — Now practice drawing this character in these smaller cells.

チ チ chi

SPEAK Pronounced just like the 'chi' in tai-chi.

LEARN This kana is drawn with three strokes; fade, stop, fade.

Your first line is a shallow, fading curve from the upper right and down slightly to the left side. Stroke number 2 is a long horizontal line with a stop. Your third stroke should begin in the middle of the first curve and intersect with the second stroke, before curving down and to the left. Make sure that your second line is wider than the first stroke on both sides!

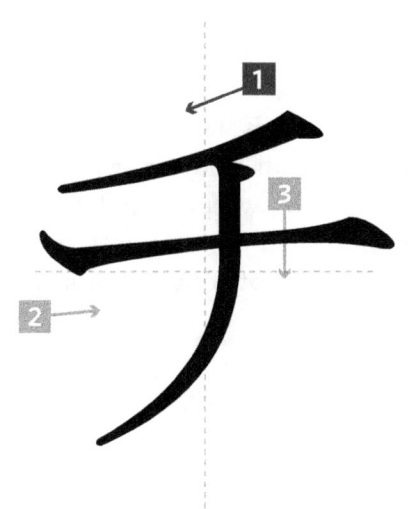

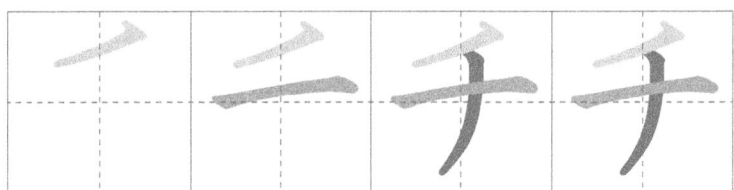

WRITE First, trace the shapes in the large cells below

PRACTICE Now practice drawing this character in these smaller cells.

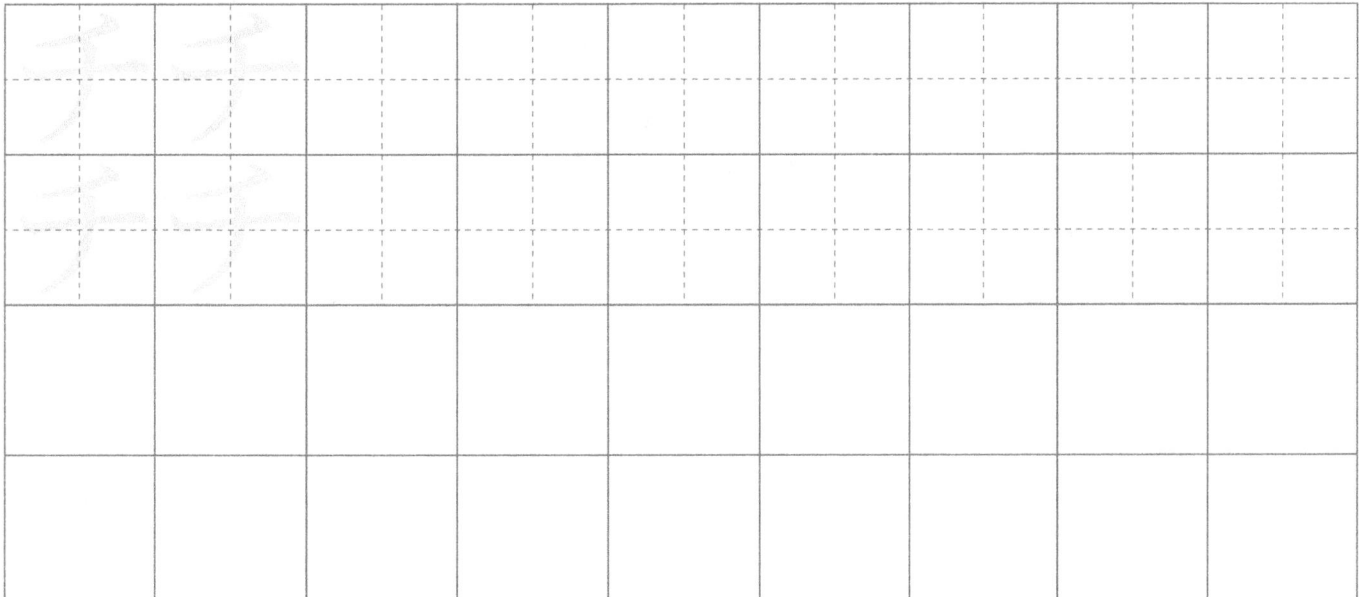

83

ツ ツ tsu

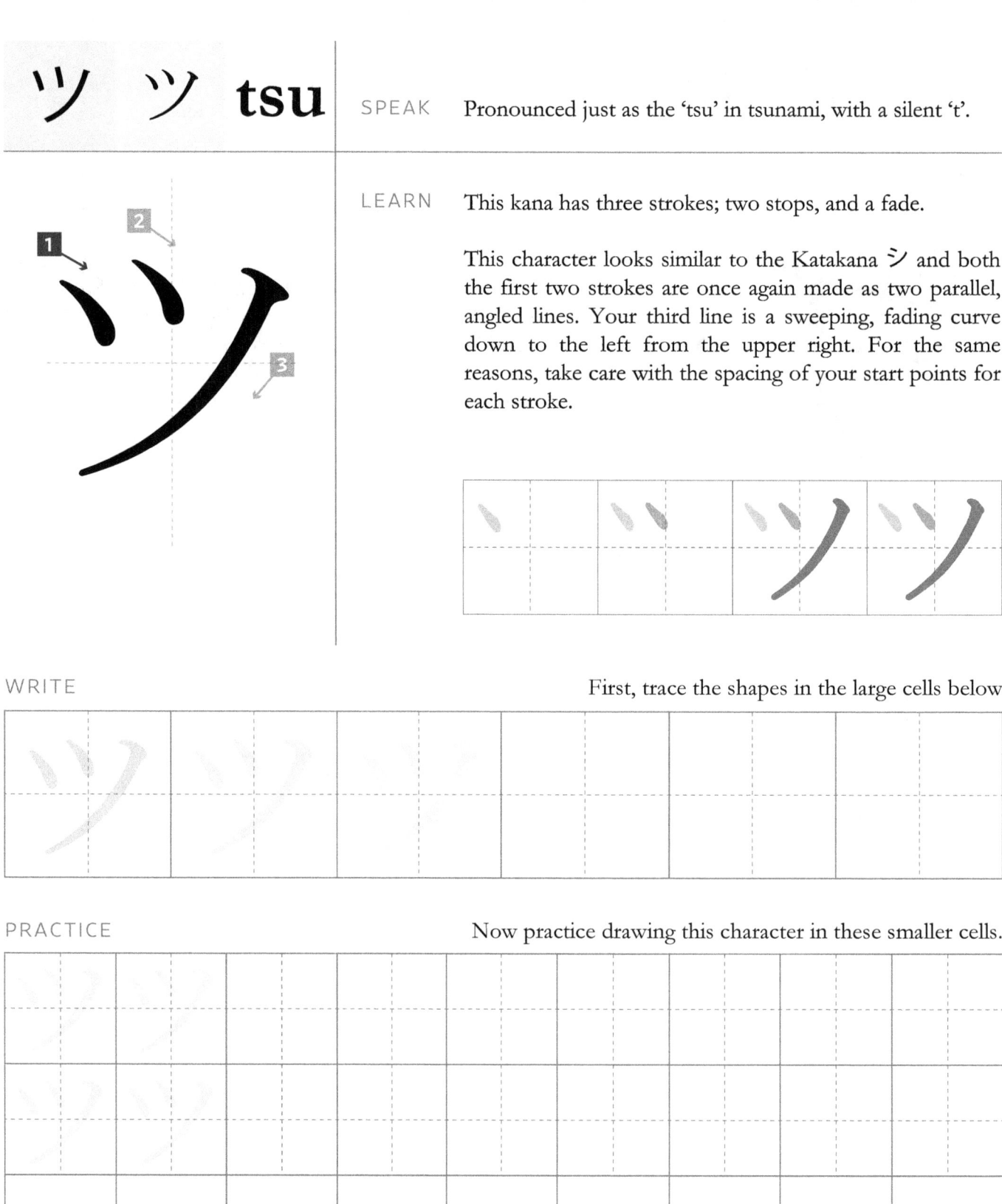

SPEAK Pronounced just as the 'tsu' in tsunami, with a silent 't'.

LEARN This kana has three strokes; two stops, and a fade.

This character looks similar to the Katakana シ and both the first two strokes are once again made as two parallel, angled lines. Your third line is a sweeping, fading curve down to the left from the upper right. For the same reasons, take care with the spacing of your start points for each stroke.

WRITE First, trace the shapes in the large cells below

PRACTICE Now practice drawing this character in these smaller cells.

テ テ **te**

SPEAK — Pronounced like the 'te' in ten.

LEARN — This kana is drawn with three strokes; stop, stop, fade.

This kana starts with two parallel stop strokes, making horizontal lines from left to right. Make sure that your second line is longer than the first. Your third mark is a shorter, curved diagonal line down and to the left side. It starts at the midpoint of your second stroke.

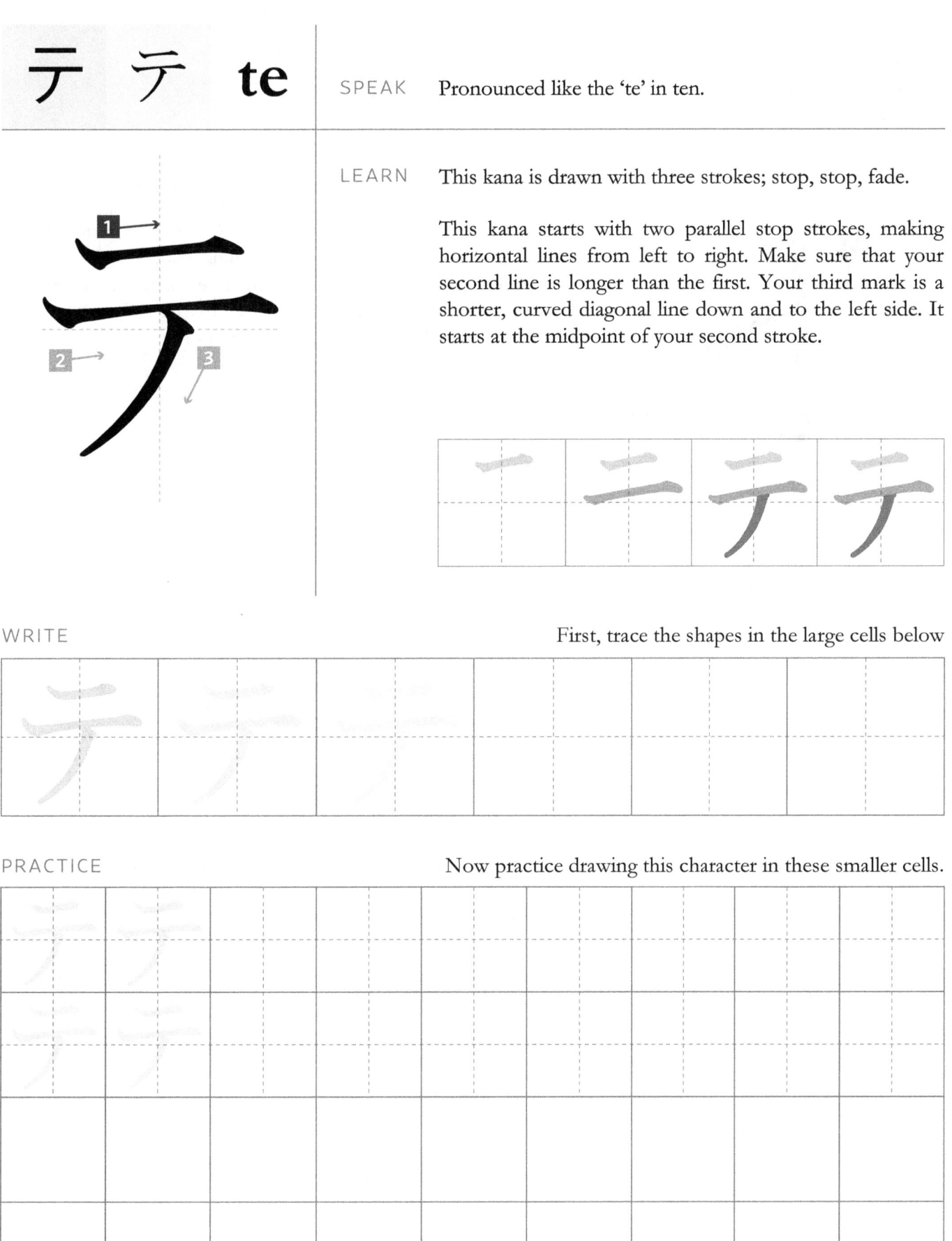

WRITE — First, trace the shapes in the large cells below

PRACTICE — Now practice drawing this character in these smaller cells.

85

ト ト **to**

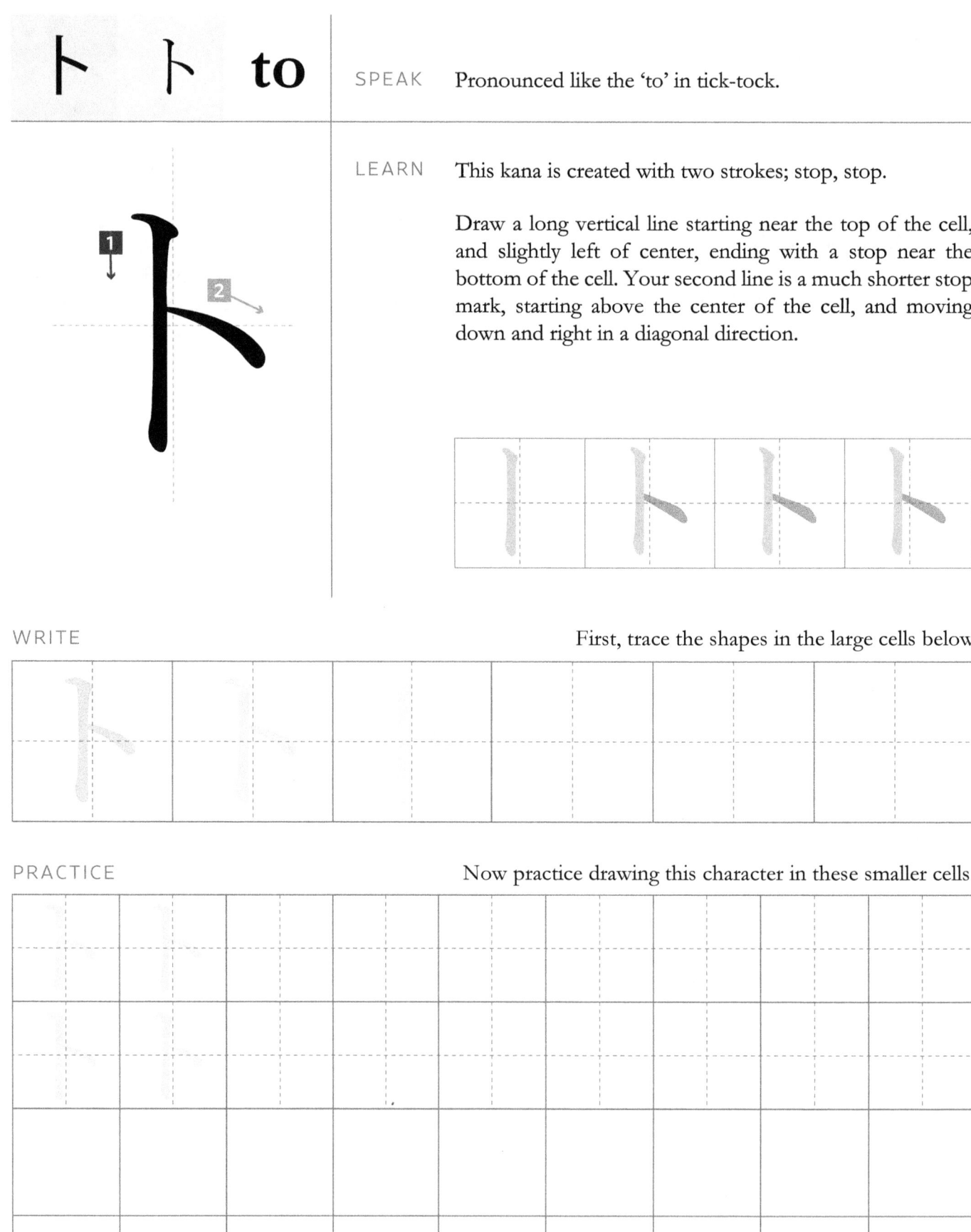

SPEAK — Pronounced like the 'to' in tick-tock.

LEARN — This kana is created with two strokes; stop, stop.

Draw a long vertical line starting near the top of the cell, and slightly left of center, ending with a stop near the bottom of the cell. Your second line is a much shorter stop mark, starting above the center of the cell, and moving down and right in a diagonal direction.

WRITE — First, trace the shapes in the large cells below

PRACTICE — Now practice drawing this character in these smaller cells.

SPEAK — Pronounced like the 'na' in narwhal.

LEARN — This kana has two strokes; a stop, and a fade.

Start with a relatively long horizontal stop stroke, above the center line. The second line begins near the top, in the middle, and is drawn down and through the first stroke. It starts as a vertical line and curves out to the lower left of the cell after the intersection.

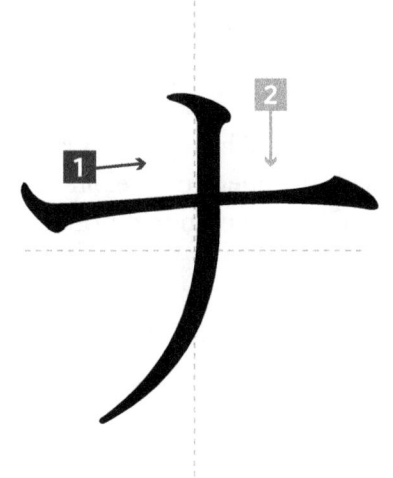

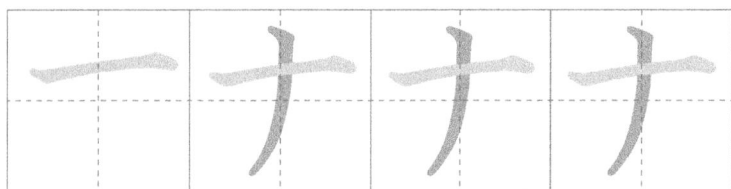

WRITE — First, trace the shapes in the large cells below

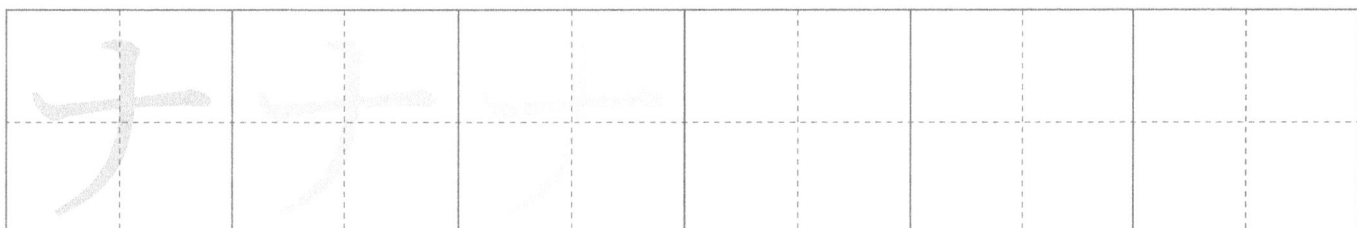

PRACTICE — Now practice drawing this character in these smaller cells.

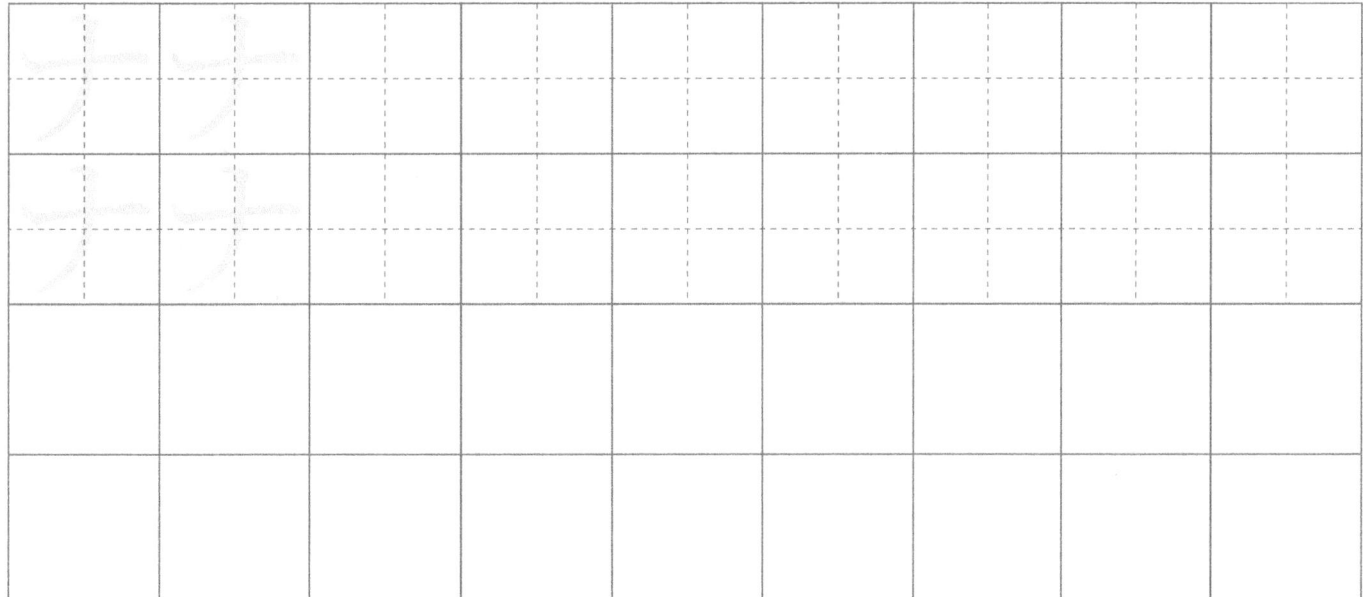

ニ　ニ　ni

SPEAK — Pronounced like the 'nee' in needle, but shorter.

LEARN — This kana has two strokes; both are stops.

As one of the more simple of the Katakana symbols, we draw ニ with two parallel lines. Each moves horizontally from left to right, with a slight incline. Your second stroke should be longer than your first, extending on both sides.

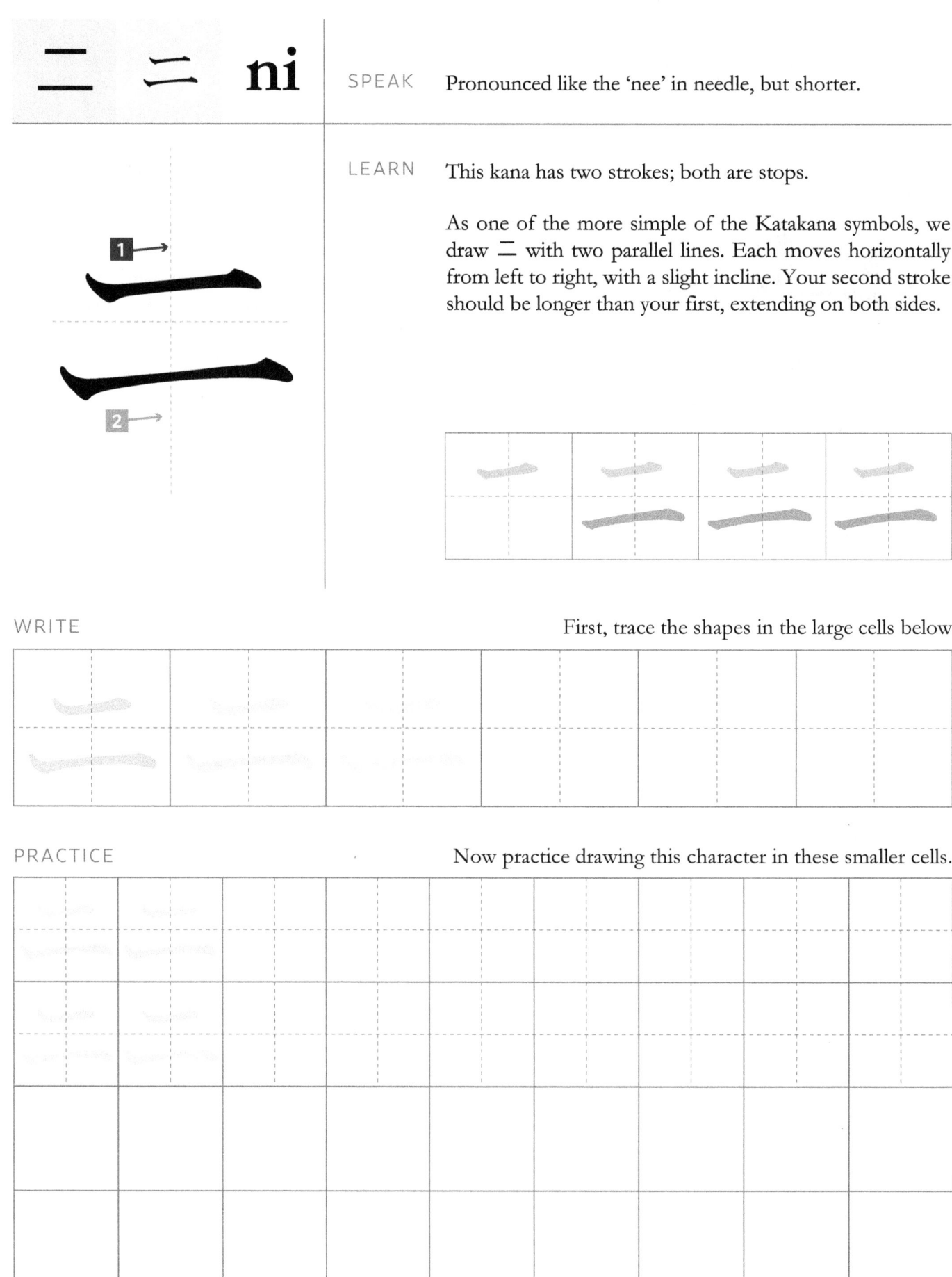

WRITE — First, trace the shapes in the large cells below

PRACTICE — Now practice drawing this character in these smaller cells.

ヌ ヌ **nu**

SPEAK Pronounced like the 'noo' in noodles but short.

LEARN Drawn with two strokes; a long fade, stop.

Begin your first stroke with a slightly inclined horizontal line from left to right and up just a little. Without lifting the pen, make a sharp turn down into a long sweeping curve. It ends as a fade in the bottom left part of the cell. Your second mark is a shorter curve that ends with a stop. It begins below the start of your first stroke and cuts through the middle of the curve you just made.

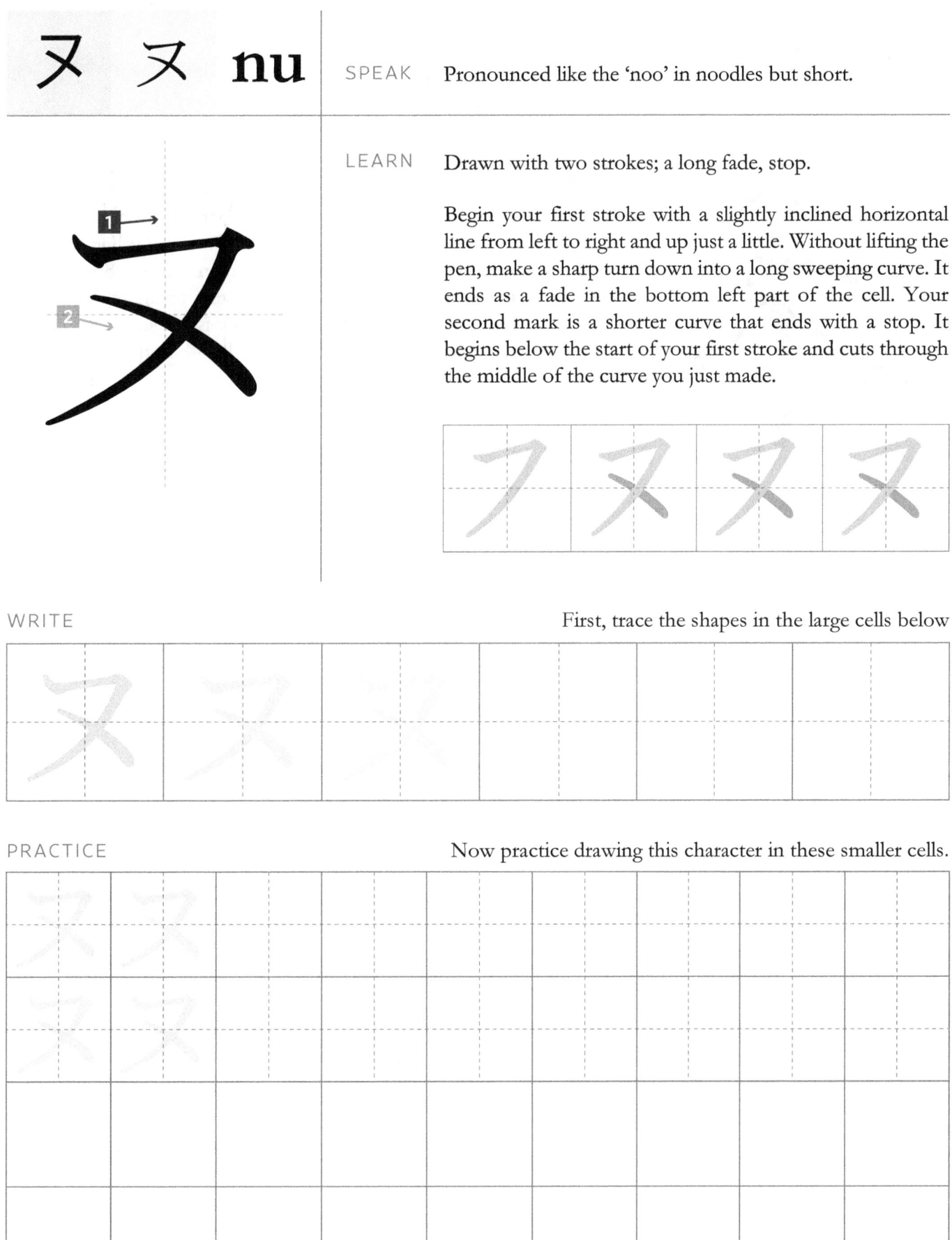

WRITE First, trace the shapes in the large cells below

PRACTICE Now practice drawing this character in these smaller cells.

89

ネ ネ **ne**

SPEAK · Pronounced like the 'ne' in nest.

LEARN · This kana has four strokes; stop, fade, stop and stop.

Begin with a short angled stop mark in the upper center. Your second mark starts with a horizontal line before a sharp turn into a fading curve down and left. Stroke three is a vertical line with a stop, starting in the middle of the curve in stroke 2. The final mark is a short diagonal line that should be roughly the same length as the lower end of your long curve.

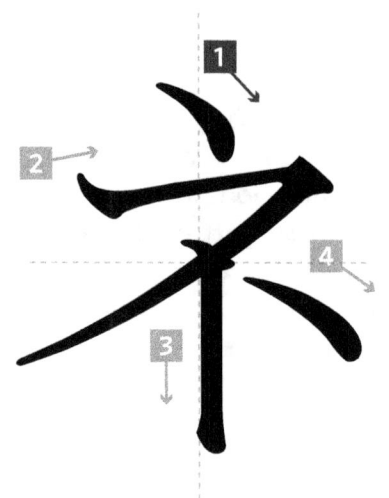

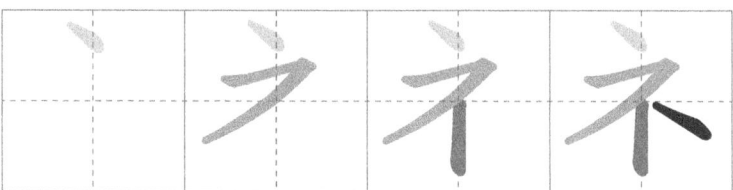

WRITE — First, trace the shapes in the large cells below

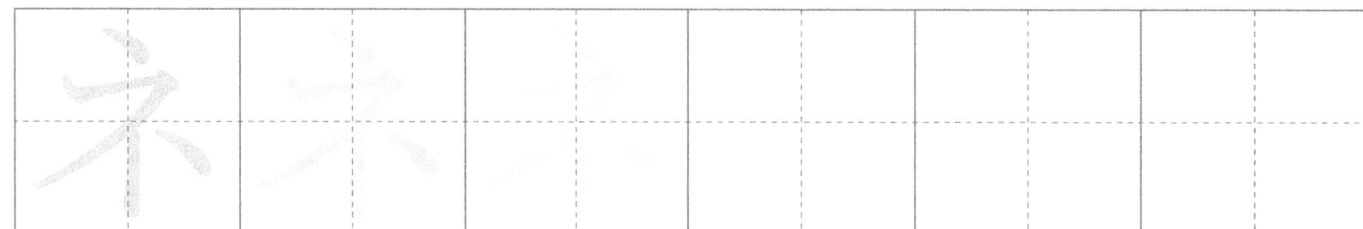

PRACTICE — Now practice drawing this character in these smaller cells.

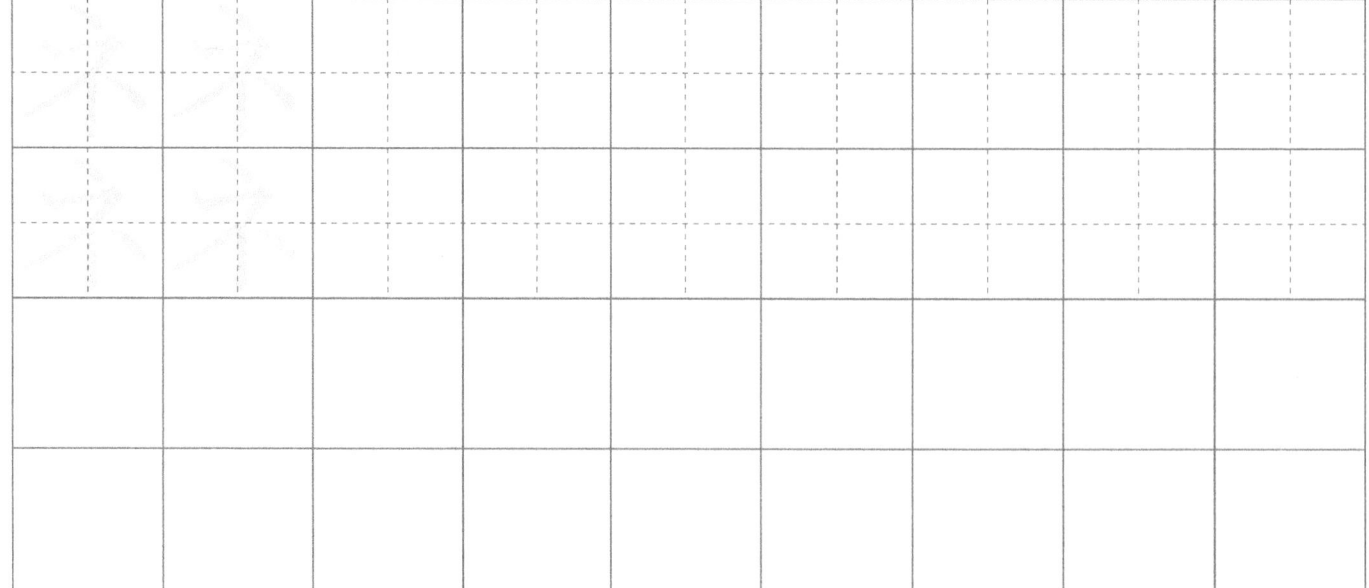

ノ ノ **no**

SPEAK — Pronounced like the 'no' in nose.

LEARN — This kana is written with one stroke; a fade.

This is probably the most simple of the Katakana and consists of a single, fading curve stroke. Start in the upper right and sweep down to a fade in the lower left. Mind the positioning of this kana.

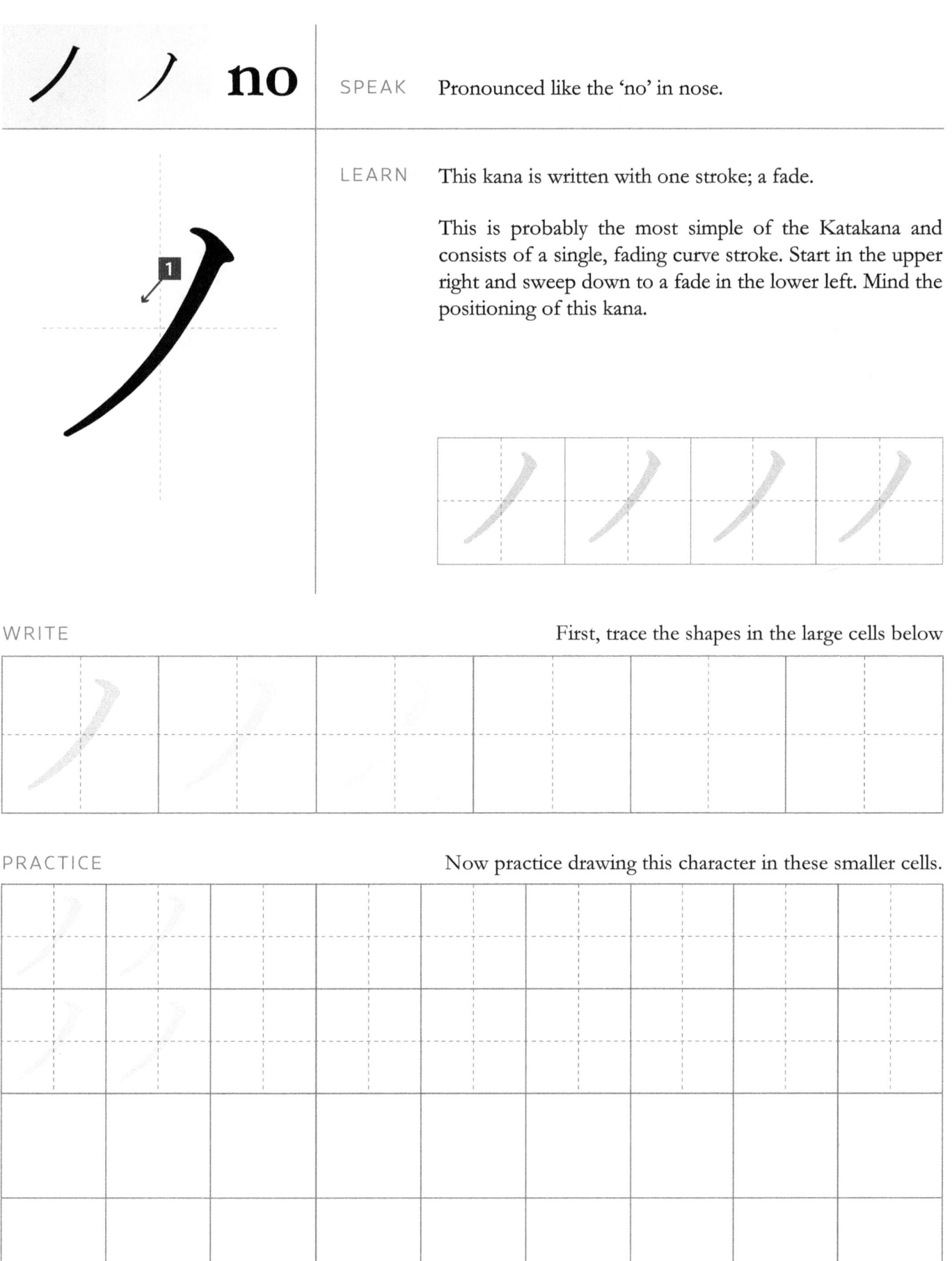

WRITE — First, trace the shapes in the large cells below

PRACTICE — Now practice drawing this character in these smaller cells.

91

ハ ハ ha

SPEAK — Pronounced as the 'ha' when laughing, like ha-ha.

LEARN — Draw this kana with two strokes; a fade and a stop.

Your first stroke is a curved diagonal line from just left of center and fading down to the left. The second mark almost mirrors the first, but ends with a stop in the lower right area. The start points should be spaced apart and positioned away from the center line.

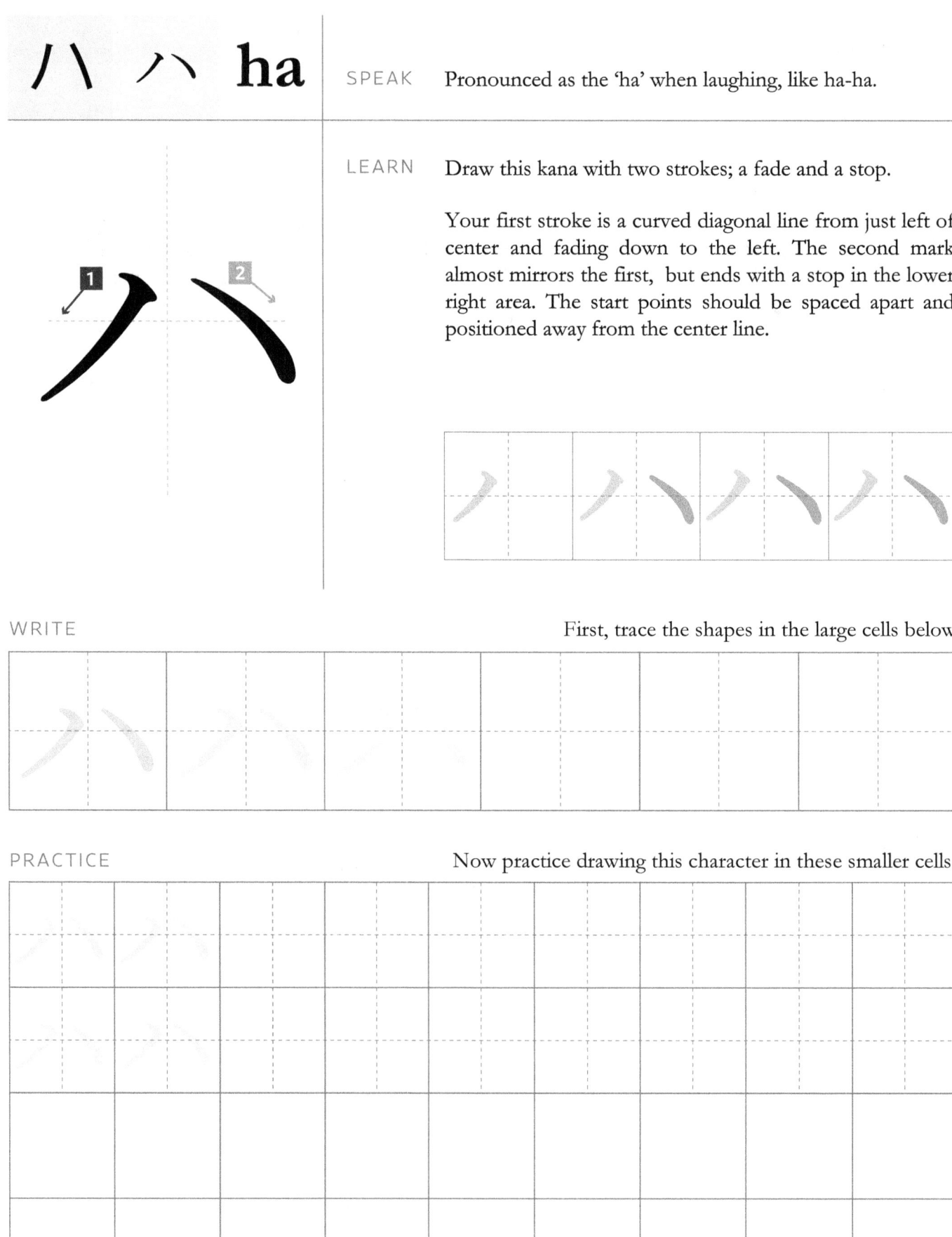

WRITE — First, trace the shapes in the large cells below

PRACTICE — Now practice drawing this character in these smaller cells.

ヒ ヒ hi

SPEAK — Pronounced like the 'he' in He or She.

LEARN — This kana is drawn with two strokes; both are stops.

Make the first stroke as a slightly angled line from left to right, ending with a stop. Your second mark begins in the upper left and starts as a vertical line downwards, just touching the end of the first. As your pen approaches the lower part of the cell, turn gently to the right - this is not a sharp angled corner like in other kana. The second stroke should come to a stop roughly below the end of your first.

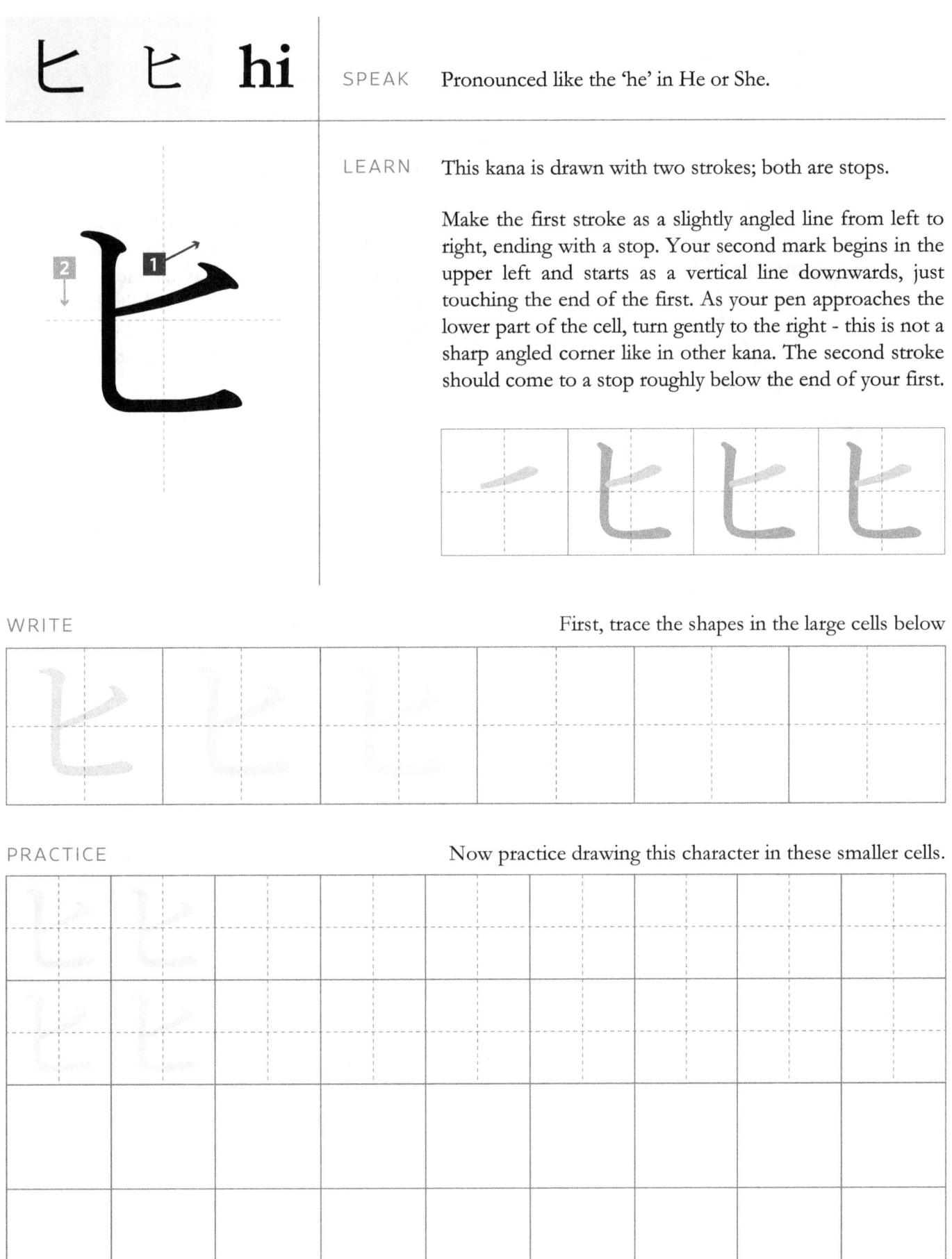

WRITE — First, trace the shapes in the large cells below

PRACTICE — Now practice drawing this character in these smaller cells.

フ フ fu

SPEAK Pronounced as 'hu' like the word 'who'.

LEARN Drawn with a single stroke; it is a long fade.

This kana has been drawn as part of the previous symbols in this workbook. With a shape similar to a *number 7*, it begins with a slightly inclined horizontal line. When your pen approaches the right side of the cell, it should turn quite sharply. Keep your pen on the page as you continue to create the long, fading curve down towards the lower left of the cell.

WRITE First, trace the shapes in the large cells below

PRACTICE Now practice drawing this character in these smaller cells.

he

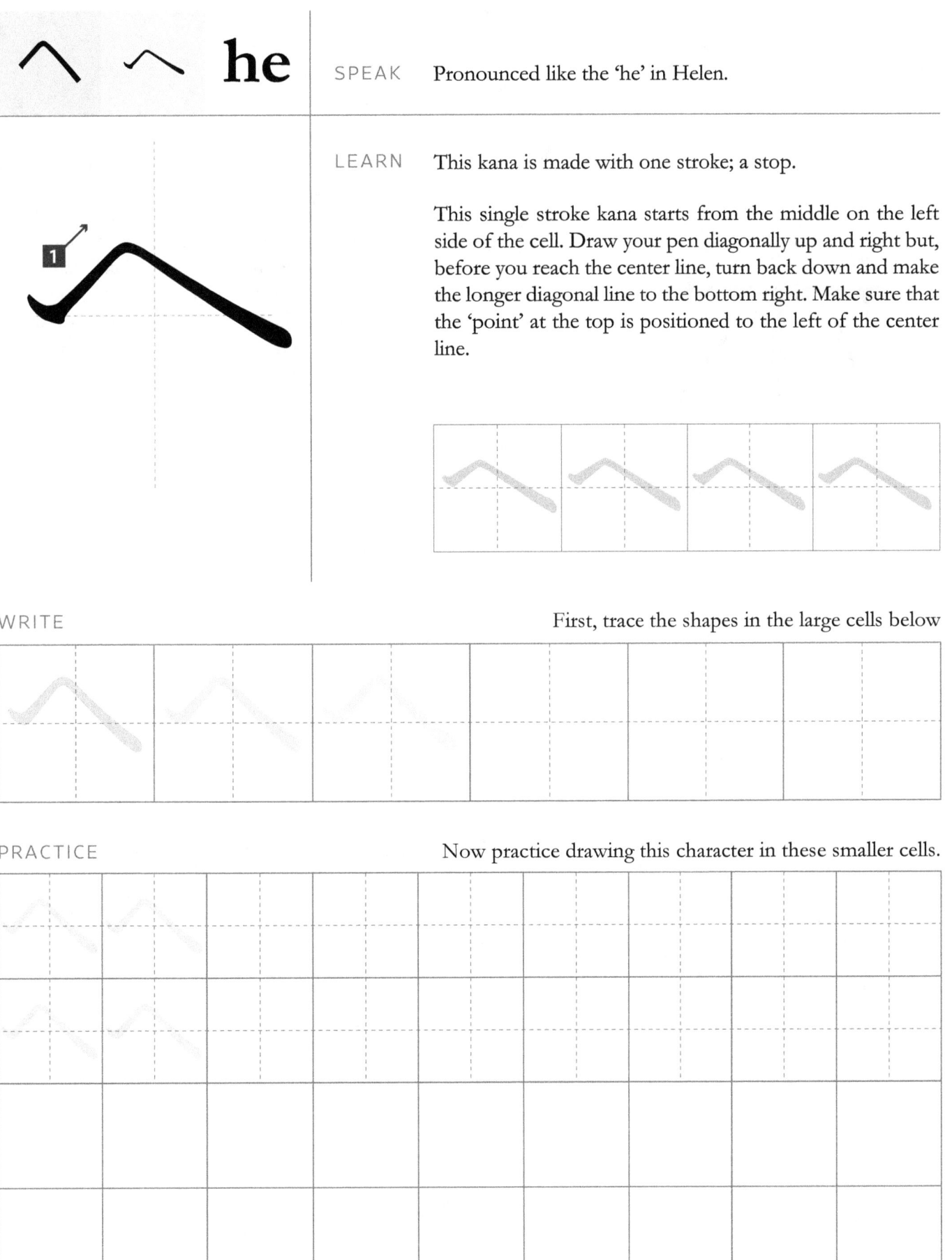

SPEAK — Pronounced like the 'he' in Helen.

LEARN — This kana is made with one stroke; a stop.

This single stroke kana starts from the middle on the left side of the cell. Draw your pen diagonally up and right but, before you reach the center line, turn back down and make the longer diagonal line to the bottom right. Make sure that the 'point' at the top is positioned to the left of the center line.

WRITE — First, trace the shapes in the large cells below

PRACTICE — Now practice drawing this character in these smaller cells.

ホ ホ ho

SPEAK — Pronounced like the 'ho' in home.

LEARN — This kana has four strokes; stop, jump fade, stop and stop.

The first stroke is a horizontal line from left to right. Your second stroke is a vertical line, cutting across the middle of the first stroke, just above the center of the cell. End with a hane by flicking your pen from the paper. The third and fourth strokes are made in the same way that we draw the kana ハ , mirroring each other. They should not make contact with any of your other marks.

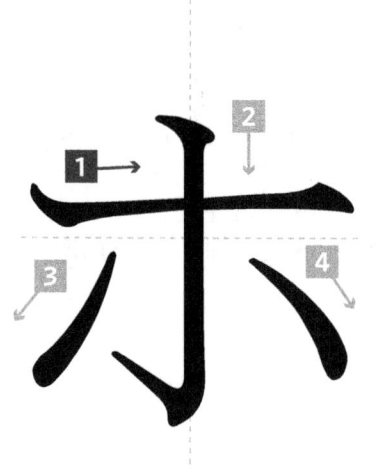

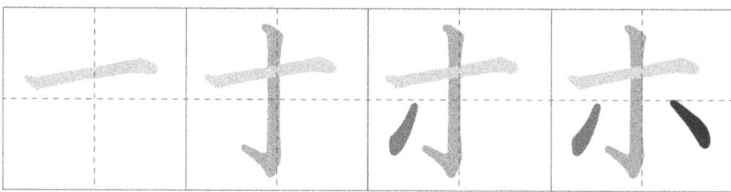

WRITE — First, trace the shapes in the large cells below

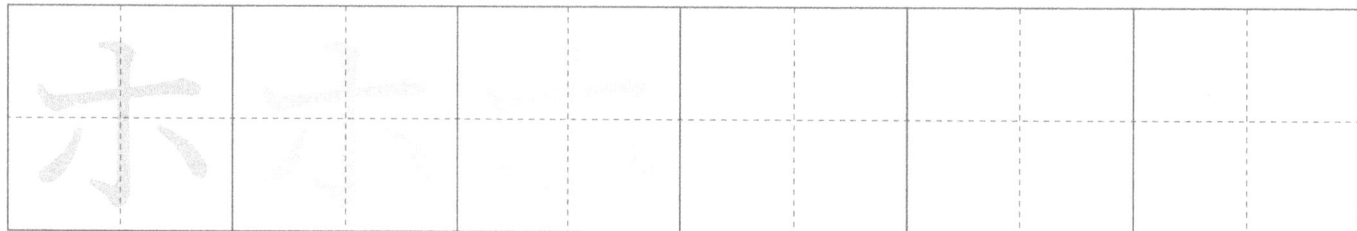

PRACTICE — Now practice drawing this character in these smaller cells.

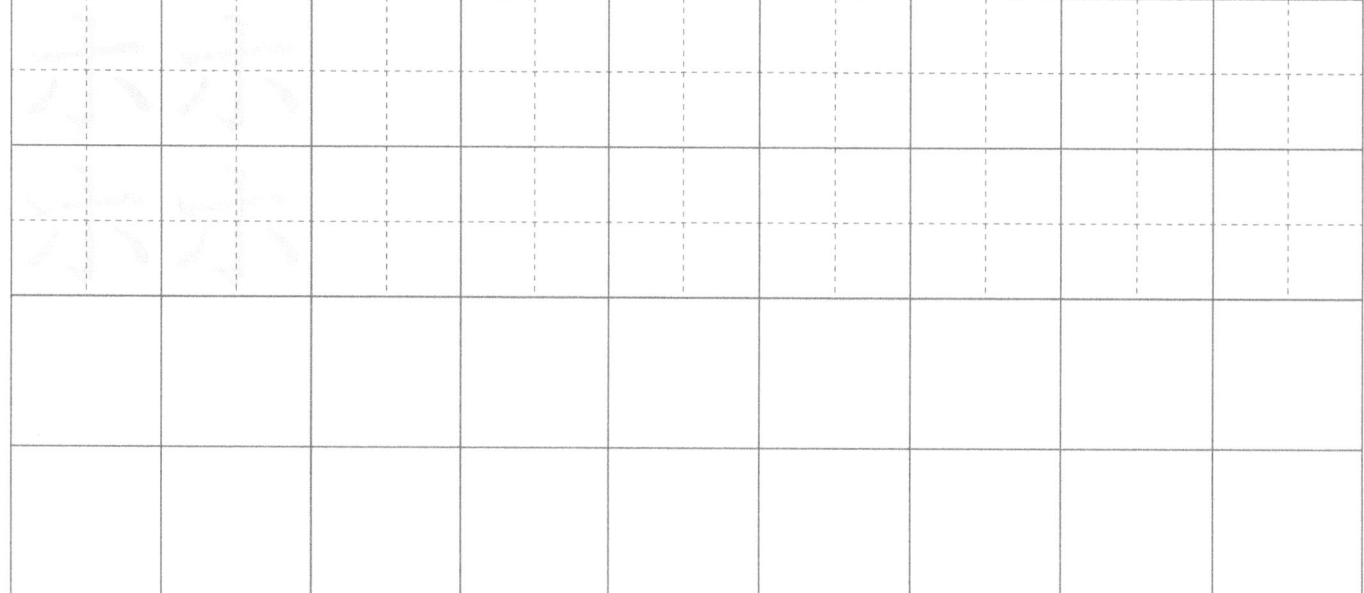

マ マ ma

SPEAK Pronounced like the 'ma' in market.

LEARN Drawn with two strokes; long fade, short stop.

Beginning with a familiar first stroke, draw your pen across the cell in a horizontal line. Without lifting your pen, turn sharply back and down with a shorter faded curve to the left. Your second stroke is a relatively short line, made at an angle down and to the right. Take care not to confuse this with the kana ア that we learned at the beginning!

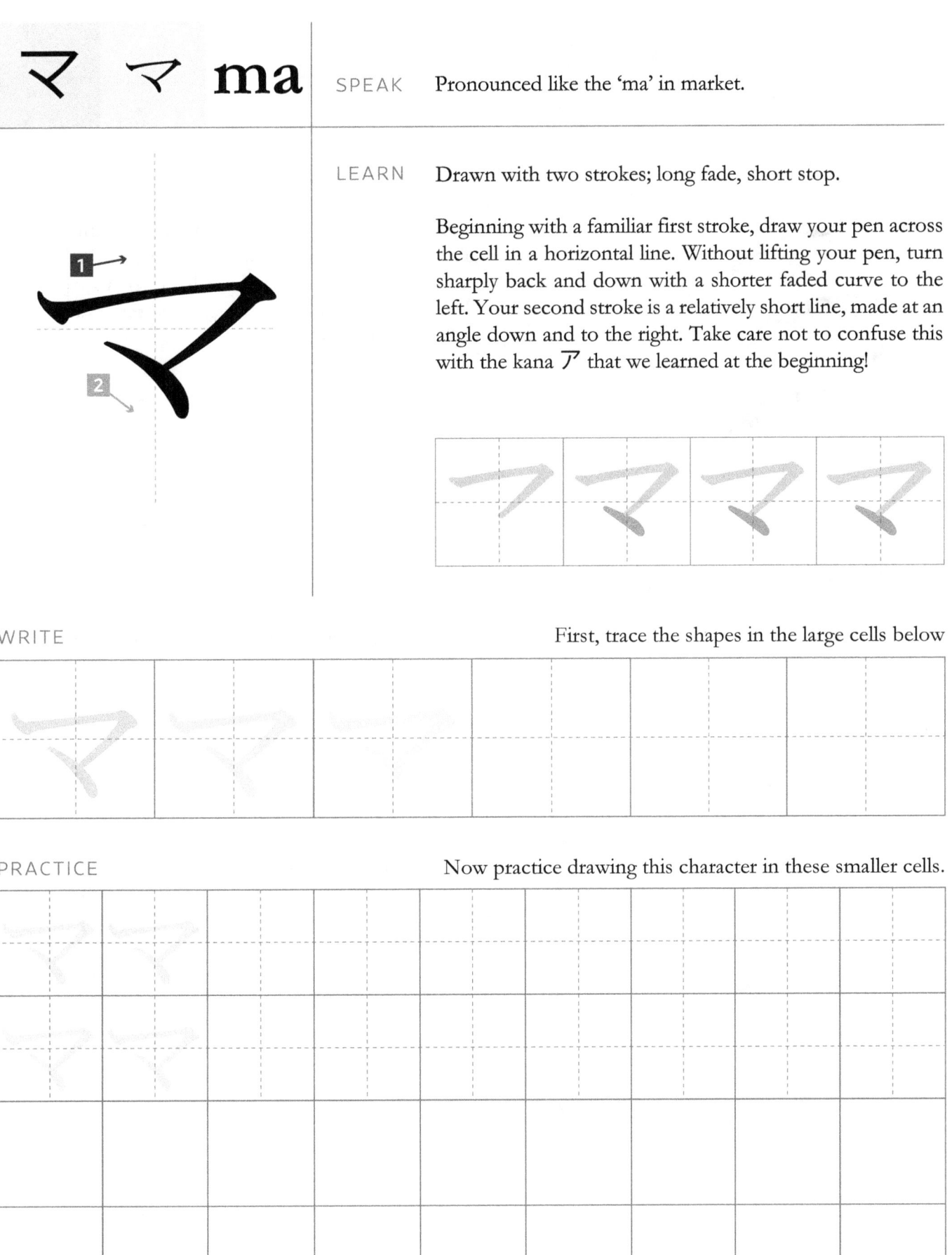

WRITE First, trace the shapes in the large cells below

PRACTICE Now practice drawing this character in these smaller cells.

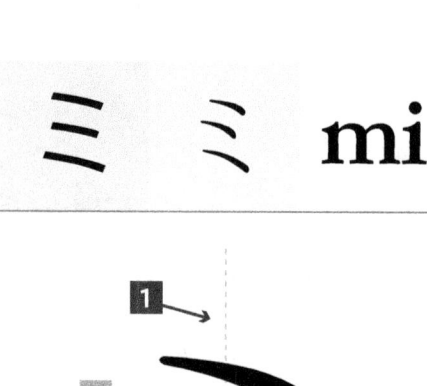

SPEAK Pronounced just like 'me'.

LEARN Drawn with three strokes; each is a short stop.

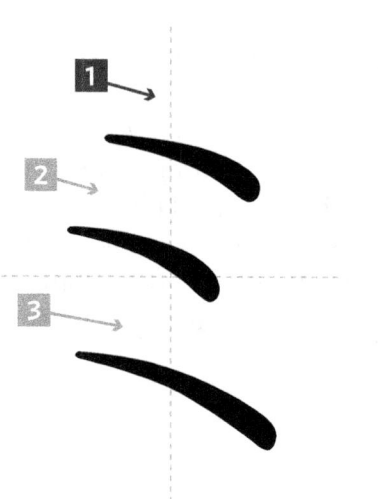

This kana is relatively simple, consisting of three short, parallel lines. Each is drawn at a slight angle, bringing your pen to a stop as you move down from left to right. The third stroke is ever so slightly longer, and the start position just a little to the right.

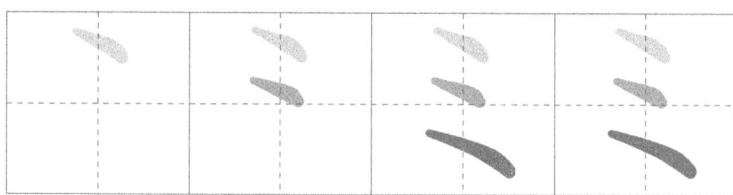

WRITE   First, trace the shapes in the large cells below

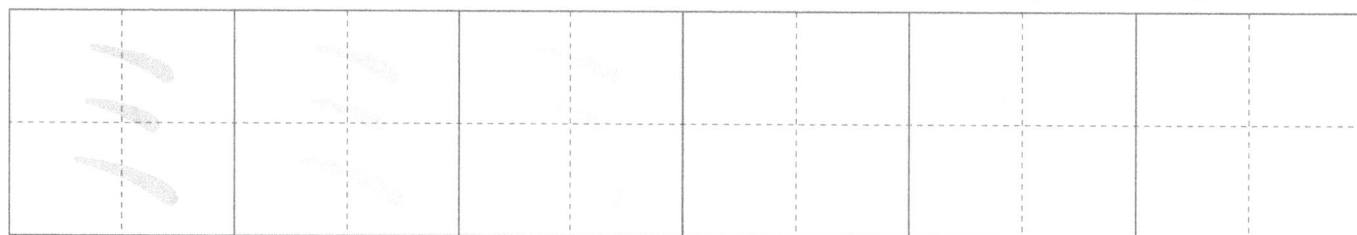

PRACTICE   Now practice drawing this character in these smaller cells.

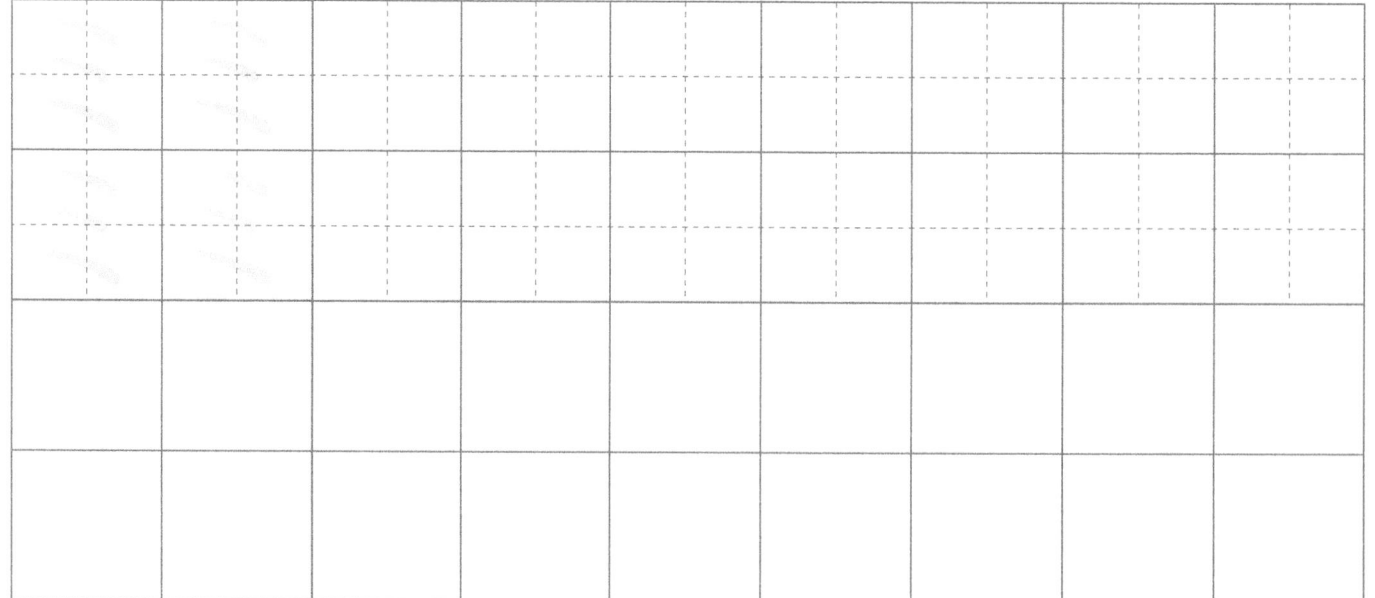

ム　ム　**mu**

SPEAK　Pronounced like 'moo' but in move.

LEARN　Draw this kana with two strokes; stop and stop.

It almost looks like three separate strokes, but the first creates a sort of L-shape. Begin with a straight line, drawn diagonally from the upper middle to the lower left. Keep your pen on the paper and make a sharp turn to the right. Move across the cell at a much more shallow angle and end with a stop. The second line is a short diagonal stop mark that should touch the end of the first stroke as it descends.

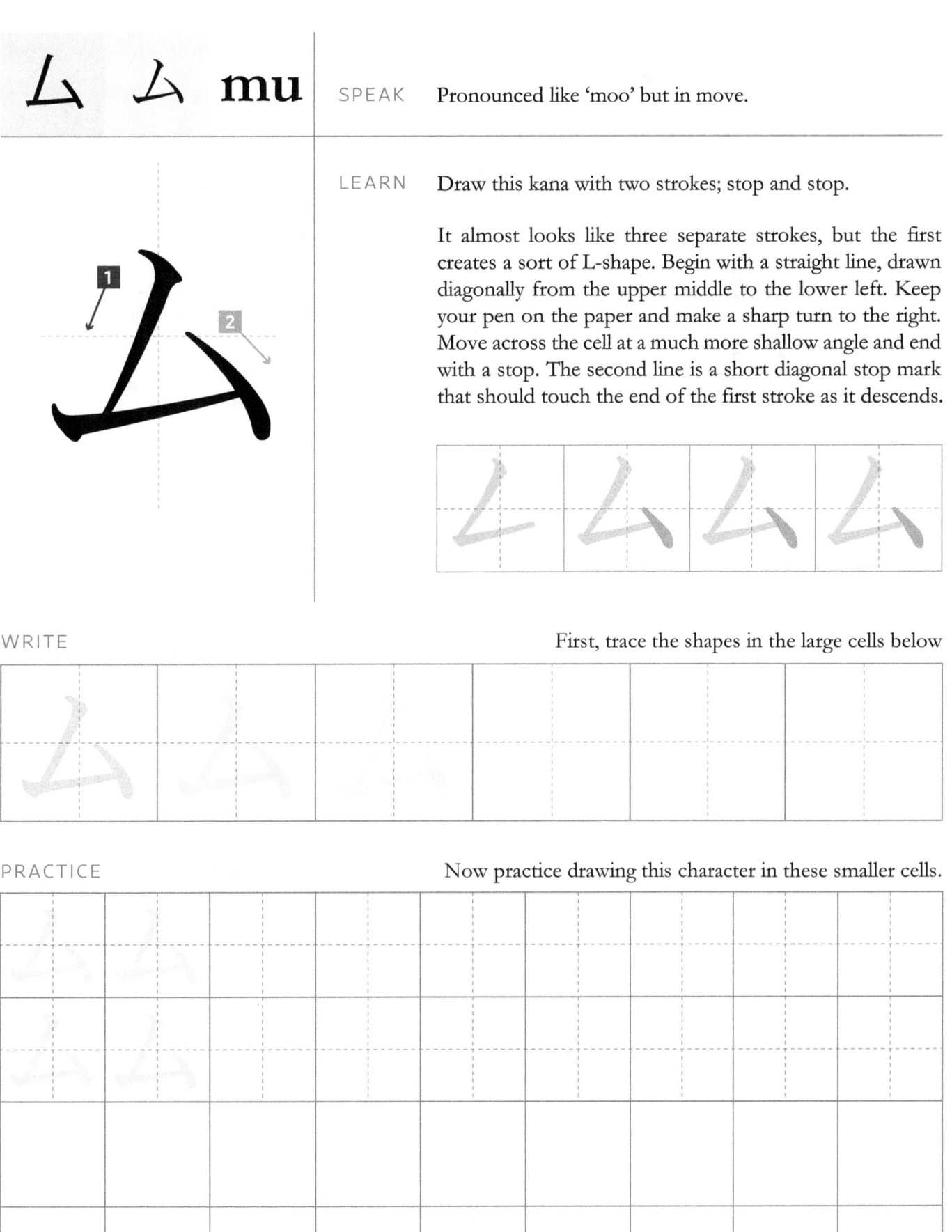

WRITE　First, trace the shapes in the large cells below

PRACTICE　Now practice drawing this character in these smaller cells.

99

メ メ **me**

SPEAK   Pronounced as 'meh' like the 'me' in mend.

LEARN   This kana is drawn with two strokes; a fade and a stop.

Your first stroke is a relatively long curved line, drawn from the upper right quadrant to the lower left. This line should end with a fade. The second diagonal mark is a shorter curve that cuts across the middle of your first stroke and ends with a stop.

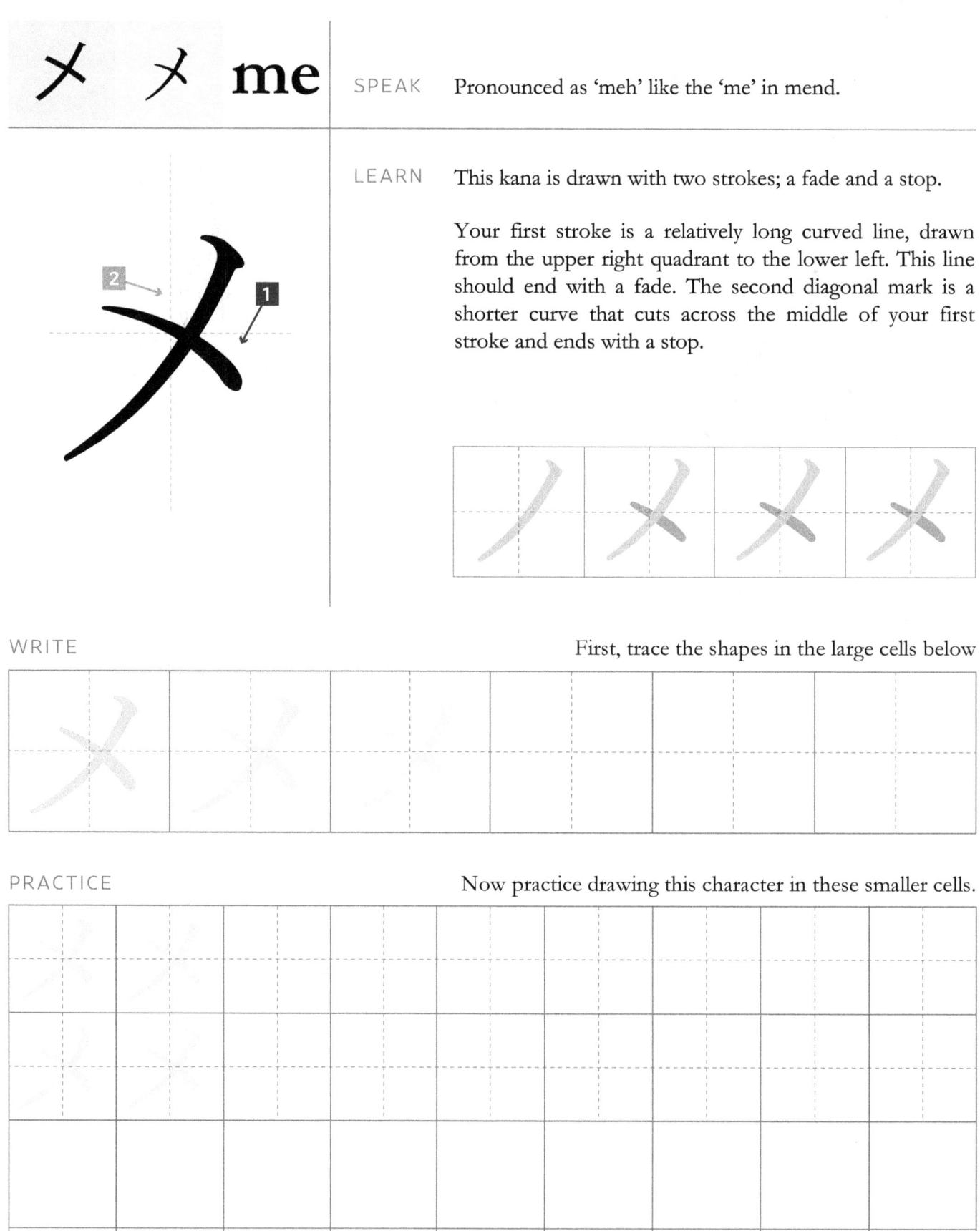

WRITE   First, trace the shapes in the large cells below

PRACTICE   Now practice drawing this character in these smaller cells.

モ も mo

SPEAK Pronounced just like the 'mo' in more.

LEARN This kana has three strokes; all of them are stops.

Start this kana by drawing the first and second strokes as two horizontal lines. The second should be a little longer than the first. Your third stroke begins on the first stroke and is drawn as a vertical line downwards, to begin with. It will cut through your second stroke and, as your pen approaches the bottom of the cell, turn gently to the right and across to a stop on the right.

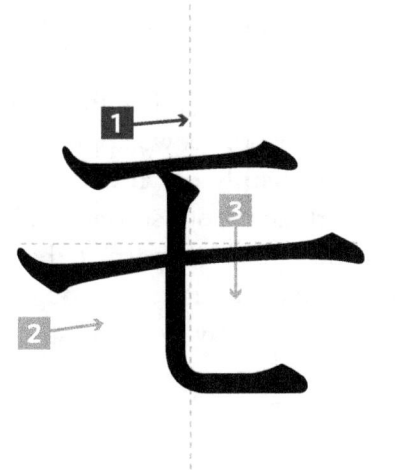

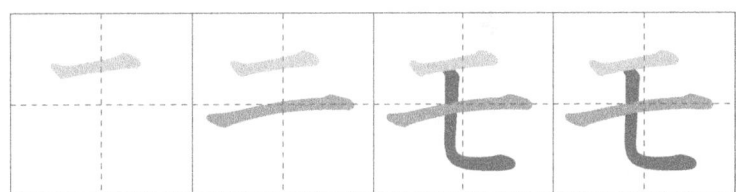

WRITE First, trace the shapes in the large cells below

PRACTICE Now practice drawing this character in these smaller cells.

ヤ ヤ **ya**

SPEAK   Pronounced like the 'ya' in yard'

LEARN   Draw this kana with two strokes; a fade and a stop.

We begin drawing this kana with a straight line from left to right, at a relatively shallow angle up. As we approach the right side of the cell, it turns sharply down and back in towards the center with a short fade. Your second stroke is a long diagonal line from the upper left part of the cell, closer to the center than the side, and it cuts through the first stroke roughly one third of the way from the start.

WRITE   First, trace the shapes in the large cells below

PRACTICE   Now practice drawing this character in these smaller cells.

ユ ユ yu

SPEAK — Pronounced like the 'u' in universal.

LEARN — This kana is drawn with two strokes; both are stops.

Your first stroke begins as a short horizontal line and then makes a sharp turn down to a stop. Your second mark starts further to the left side than your first, and below the center line. It is a longer horizontal line and must touch the end of the first stroke. So that this symbol is not confused with katakana ㄱ, take care to make the second stroke extend further on both sides.

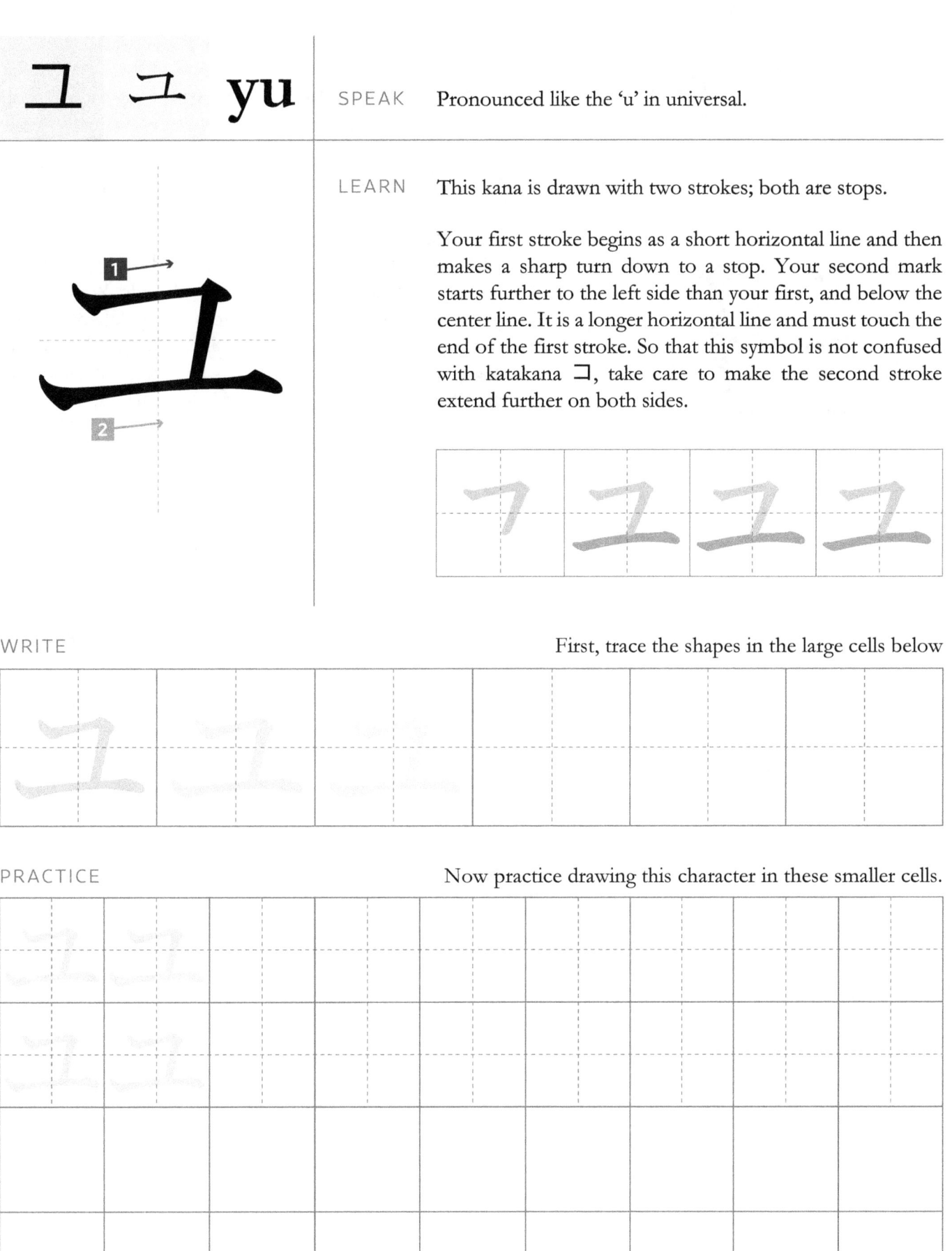

WRITE — First, trace the shapes in the large cells below

PRACTICE — Now practice drawing this character in these smaller cells.

ヨ ヨ **yo**

SPEAK Pronounced just like the 'yo' in yo-yo.

LEARN This kana is drawn with three strokes; all stops.

This kana looks like is a backwards letter E and, similar to the kana, on the previous page, starts with a horizontal line that turns into a vertical line on the right side. Your second line is slightly shorter, drawn across the middle of the cell to meet the center of the vertical line. Finally, the third line is a slightly longer one, from left to right, that meets the end of the first stroke in the lower right quadrant.

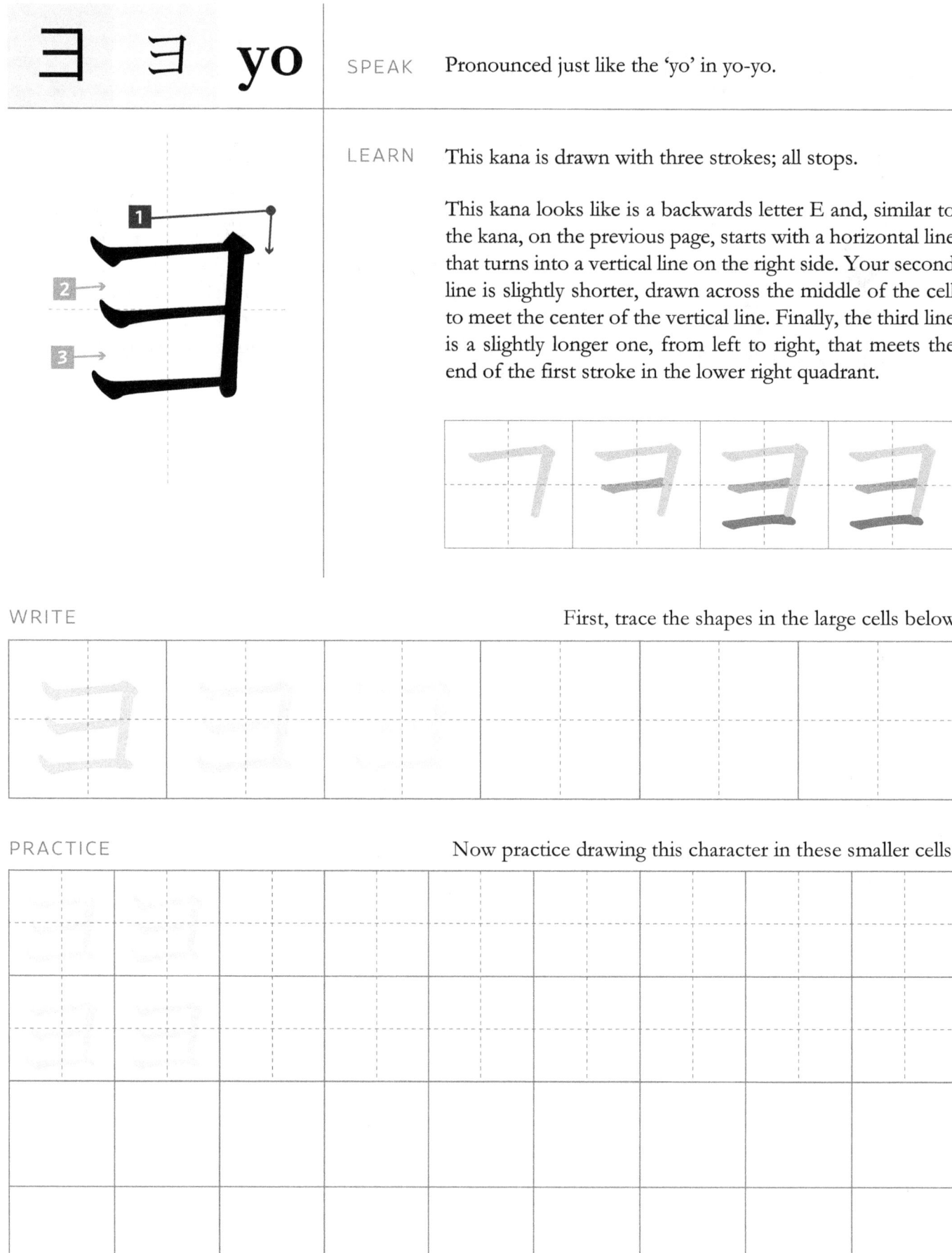

WRITE First, trace the shapes in the large cells below

PRACTICE Now practice drawing this character in these smaller cells.

ラ ラ **ra**

SPEAK	Pronounced like the 'ra' in ramen.
LEARN	This kana is drawn with two strokes; stop, fade.

Begin by making a short horizontal line with a stop stroke near the top of the cell. Stroke number two is like the *number 7 shape*, and starts with a longer, horizontal line in parallel to the first stroke. It then turns to make a long, curved diagonal line. Fade this stroke out towards the central area at the bottom.

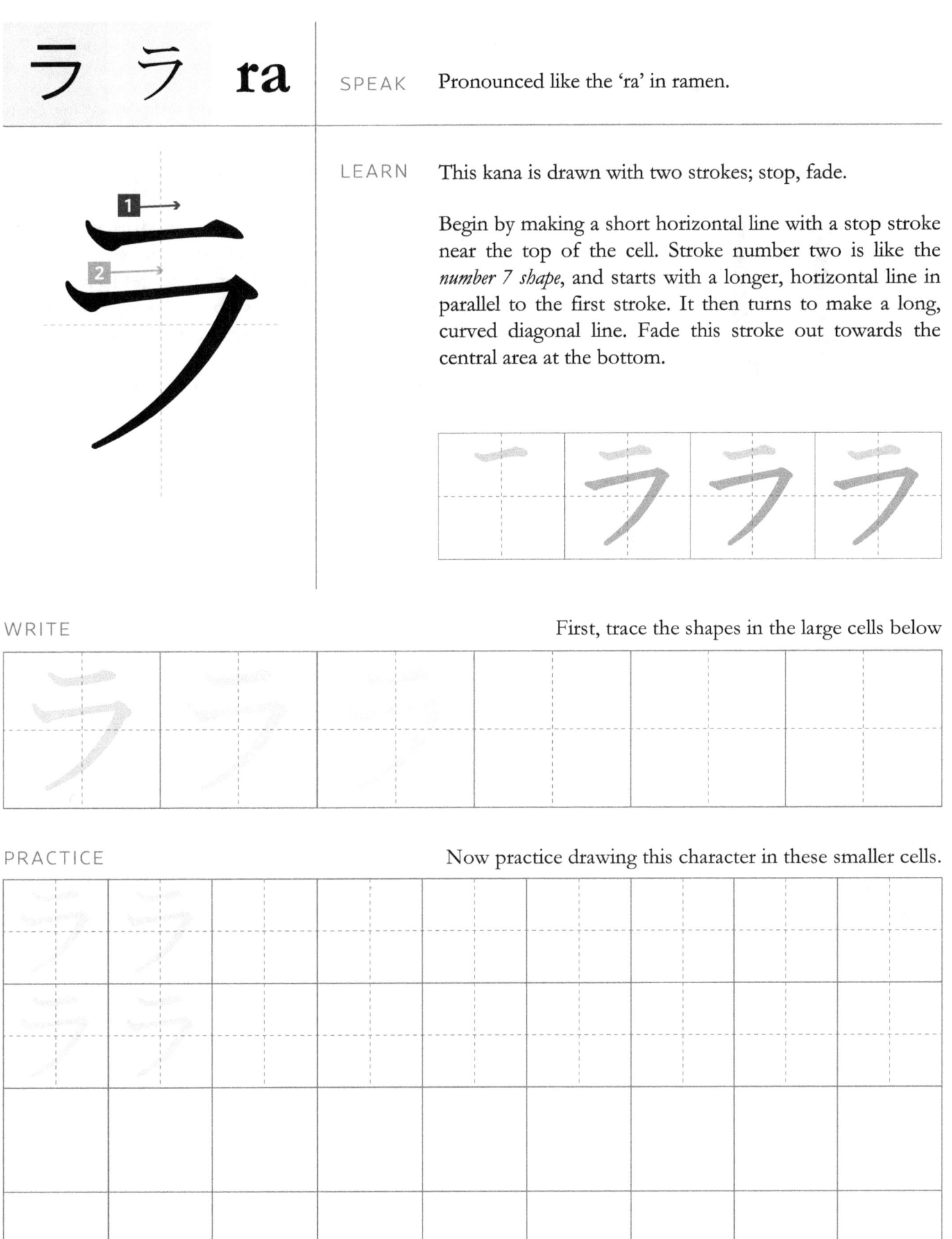

WRITE — First, trace the shapes in the large cells below

PRACTICE — Now practice drawing this character in these smaller cells.

105

リ リ ri

SPEAK — Pronounced like the 'ree' in reef.

LEARN — This kana is drawn with two strokes; stop, fade.

This is another Katakana symbol that is visually similar to the Hiragana counterpart. The first stroke is simply a straight, vertical line from the upper left area to just below the center line. It ends with a stop. Your second line starts at a similar height as the first stroke and is drawn straight down to the center line before curving back to the lower left part of the cell - end this stroke with a fade.

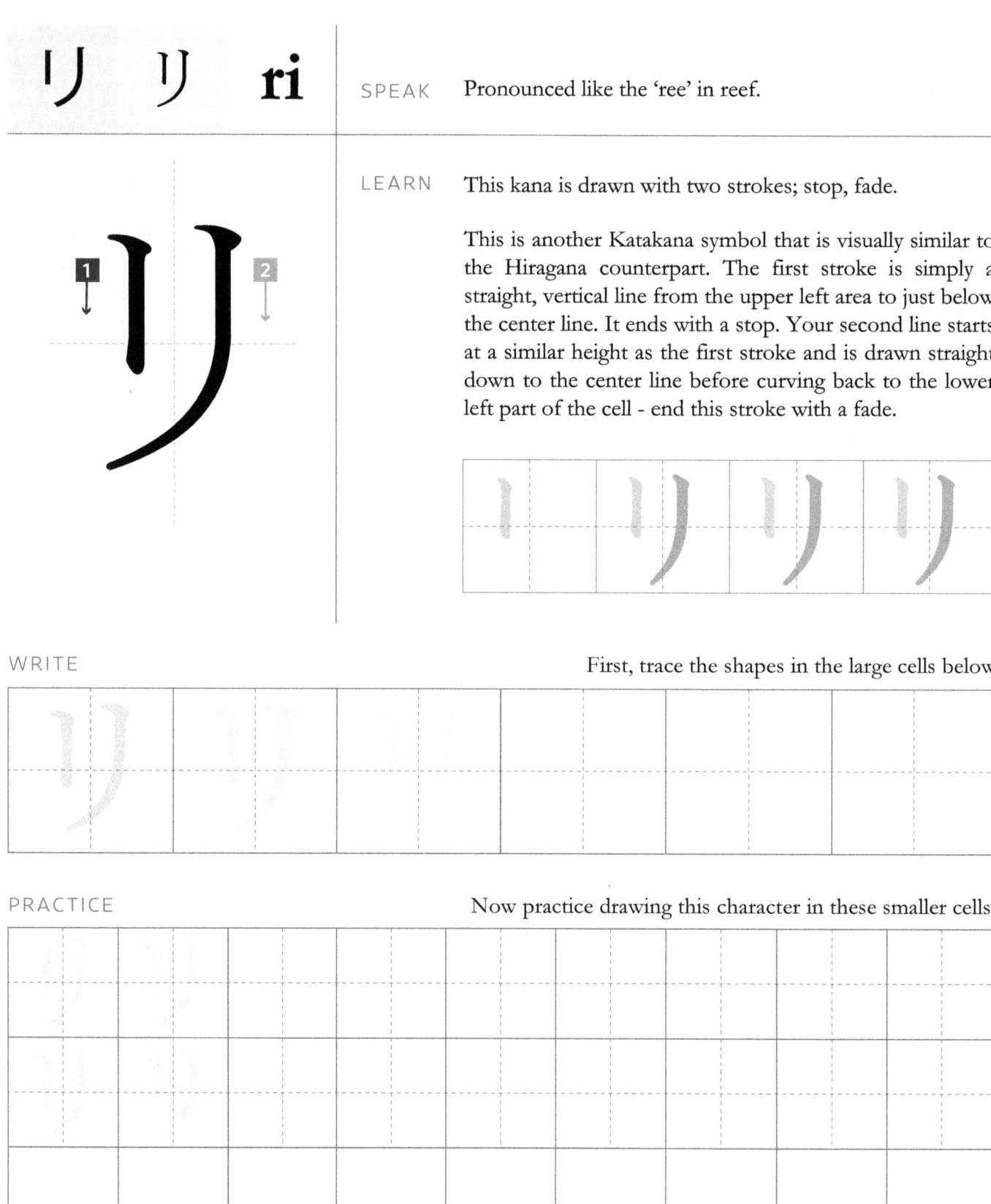

WRITE — First, trace the shapes in the large cells below

PRACTICE — Now practice drawing this character in these smaller cells.

ル ル ru

SPEAK — Pronounced like the 'rew' in brew.

LEARN — This kana is drawn with two strokes; both are fades.

Begin with a curved line from the upper area down to the lower left side and finish it with a fade. The second stroke begins as a straight vertical line from higher point than the first, and just to the right of the center line. As your pen approaches the bottom, turn sharply to the right and up with a slightly curved, fading stroke to end.

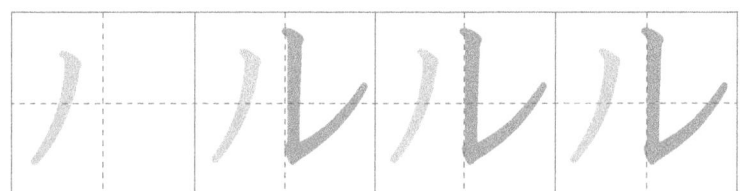

WRITE — First, trace the shapes in the large cells below

PRACTICE — Now practice drawing this character in these smaller cells.

107

レ　レ　re

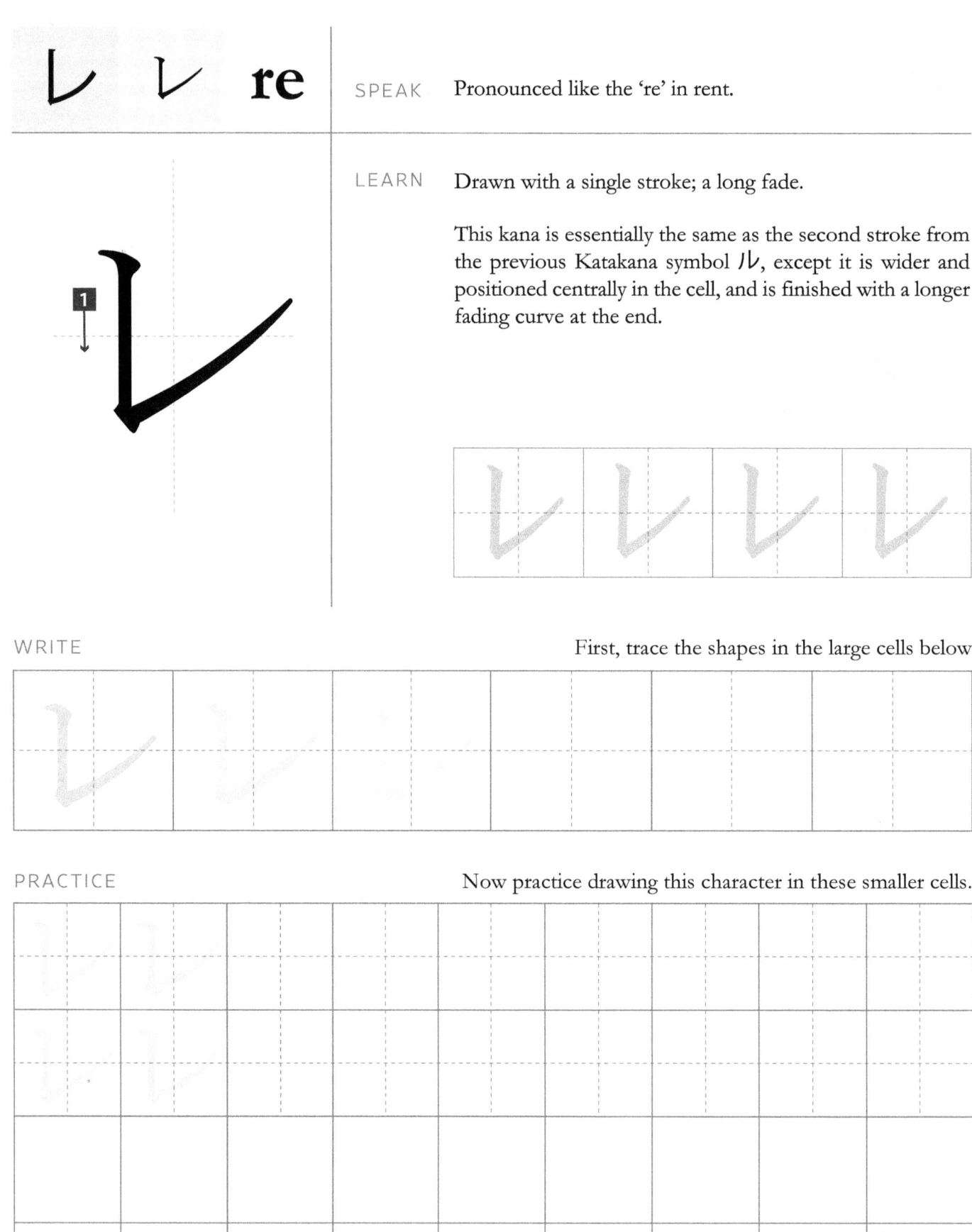

SPEAK — Pronounced like the 're' in rent.

LEARN — Drawn with a single stroke; a long fade.

This kana is essentially the same as the second stroke from the previous Katakana symbol ル, except it is wider and positioned centrally in the cell, and is finished with a longer fading curve at the end.

WRITE — First, trace the shapes in the large cells below

PRACTICE — Now practice drawing this character in these smaller cells.

ロ ro

SPEAK Pronounced like the 'ro' in road.

LEARN This kana is drawn with three strokes; all are stops.

Make your first stroke with a straight vertical line in the left half of the cell. The second stroke starts in the same place as your first, and is drawn out to the right before turning down in a straight line. The final stroke is another straight horizontal line, starting at the end of the first stroke. Finish with a stop as your pen meets the end of the second stroke. Your box shape will be positioned lower center overall.

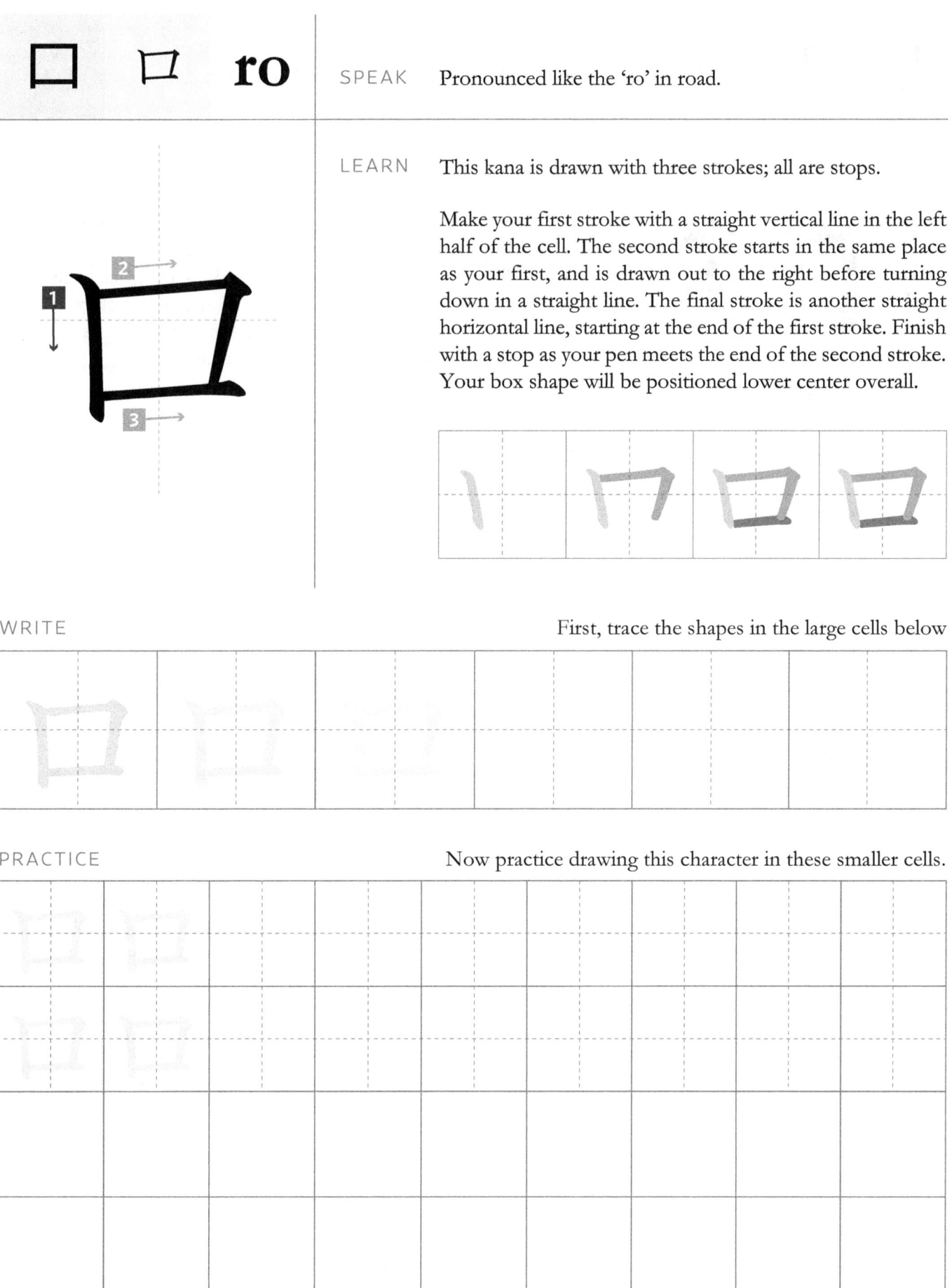

WRITE First, trace the shapes in the large cells below

PRACTICE Now practice drawing this character in these smaller cells.

109

ワ ワ **wa**

SPEAK — Pronounced like the 'wa' in wagon.

LEARN — This kana is drawn with two strokes; stop, fade.

So that this kana is not confused with Katakana ク, it's important that your first stroke makes a straight vertical line. The second stroke starts in the same place as the first stroke and moves straight out to the right before turning and becoming a curved diagonal line. Fade this stroke out as it approaches the bottom near the center.

WRITE — First, trace the shapes in the large cells below

PRACTICE — Now practice drawing this character in these smaller cells.

ヲ ヲ **wo***

SPEAK — Pronounced like the 'oh' in woah, with a silent 'w'.

LEARN — Drawn with three strokes; long fade and two stops.

Our penultimate kana symbol starts with two horizontal strokes in the upper half of the cell. They are parallel lines and the second is slightly shorter. The third stroke is a long, sweeping curve that starts at the end of the first stroke. It should meet the end of the second stroke and fade out in the lower left area of the cell.

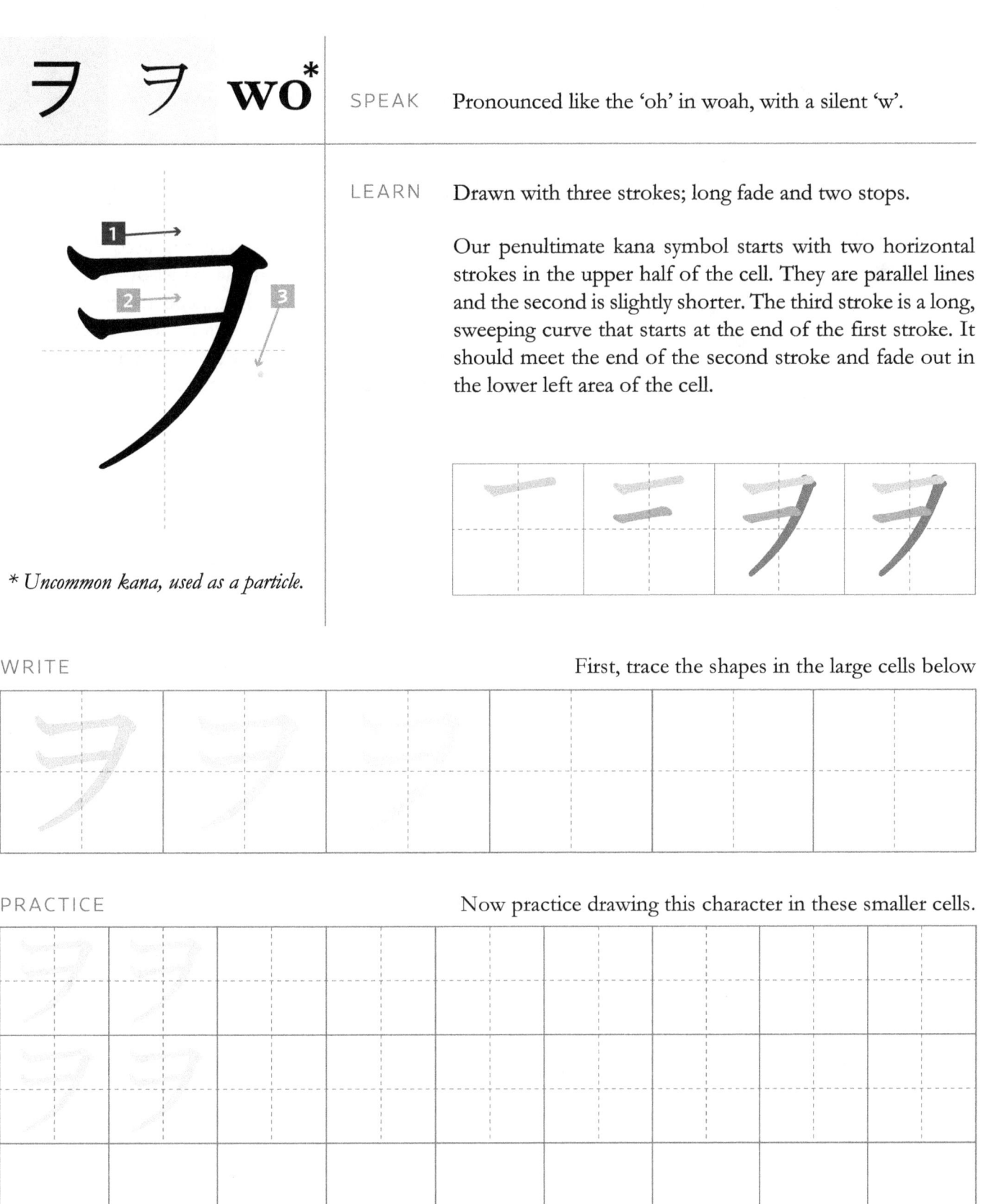

* Uncommon kana, used as a particle.

WRITE — First, trace the shapes in the large cells below

PRACTICE — Now practice drawing this character in these smaller cells.

ン ン **n**

SPEAK — Pronounced like just the 'n' sound in ink.

LEARN — This kana is drawn with two strokes; short stop, fade.

Our final basic Katakana ン is easily confused with ソ, so it is vital that the character is drawn wider overall. The first stroke is a fairly short angled line, almost vertical, ending with a stop. The second stroke is a more shallow, curved line running diagonally from the lower left and up to the top right side, ending with a fade.

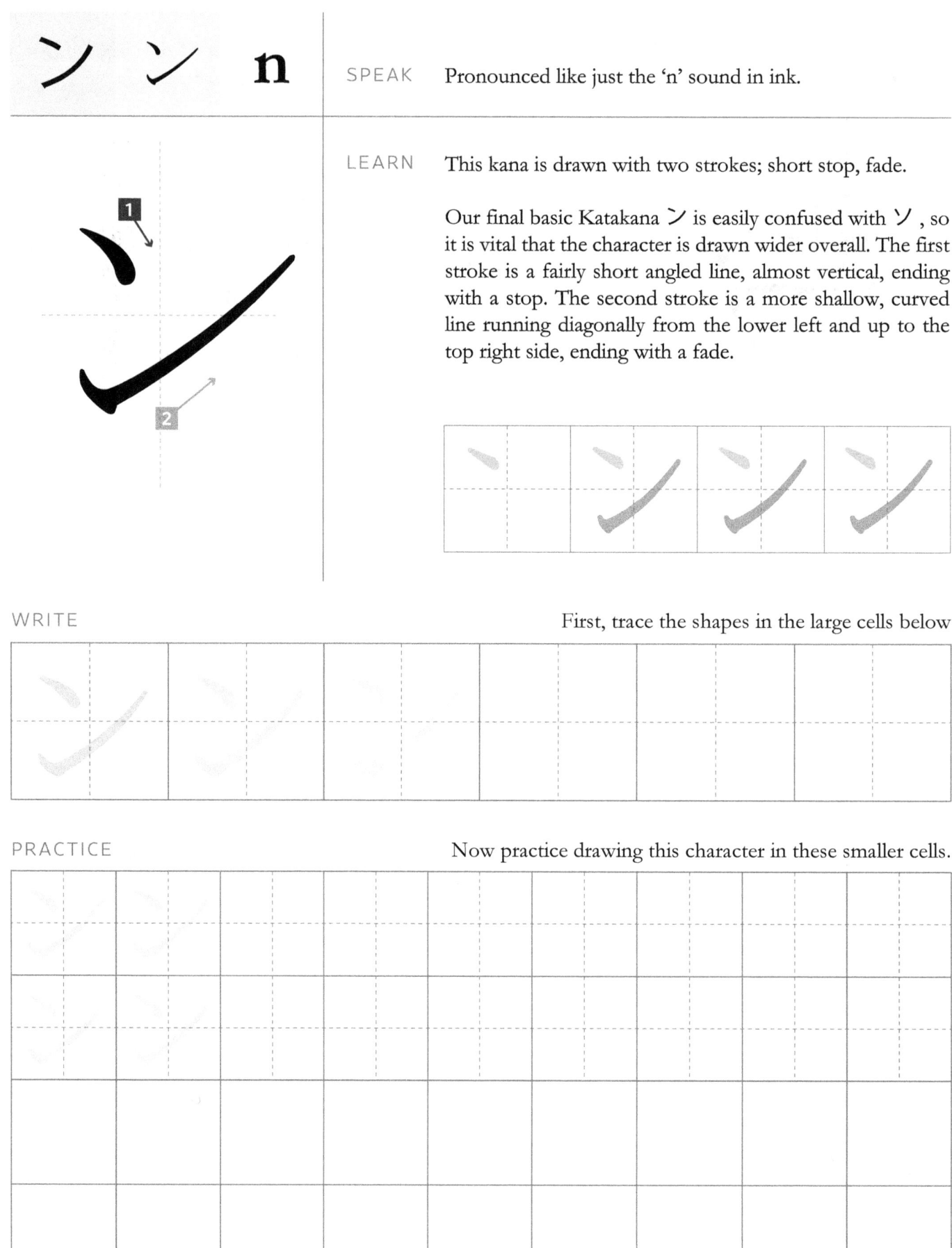

WRITE — First, trace the shapes in the large cells below

PRACTICE — Now practice drawing this character in these smaller cells.

Part 6

GENKOUYOUSHI
GRID PAPER FOR FURTHER PRACTICE

Part 7

FLASH CARDS
PHOTOCOPY OR CUT OUT & KEEP

あ	や	ま
い	を	り
つ	せ	ゆ
ぶ	へ	し

a
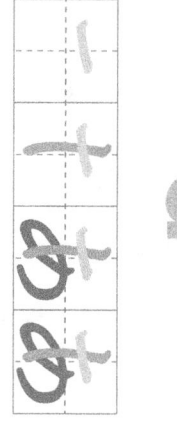
Pronounced like the 'a' in car or father, but shorter.

i
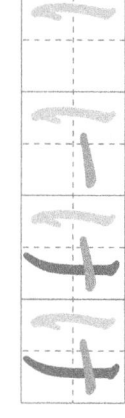
Pronounced like the 'ee' in eel.

u
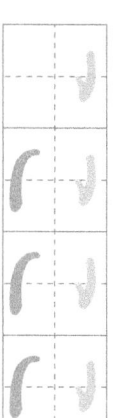
Pronounced like the 'oo' in zoo.

e
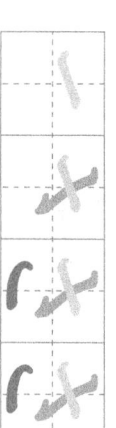
Pronounced as 'eh' like the 'e' in men.

o
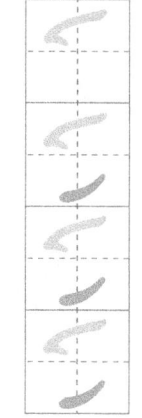
Pronounced like the 'o' in original.

ka

Pronounced like 'car' but without the 'r' sound.

ki
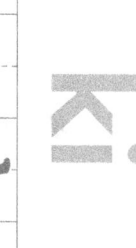
Pronounced like 'key'.

ku
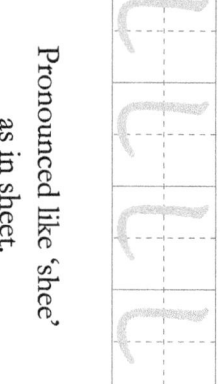
Pronounced like the 'koo' in cuckoo.

ke

Pronounced like the 'ke' in Kenneth.

ko
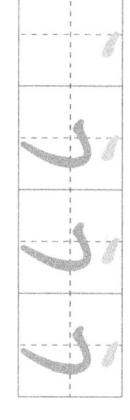
Pronounced like the 'co' in core.

sa
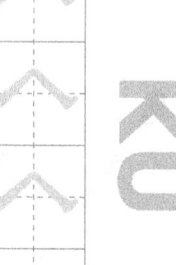
Pronounced like the 'sa' in sardines.

shi

Pronounced like 'shee' as in sheet.

す	ふ	ぁ
せ	つ	し
れ	へ	め
た	て	ぬ

su
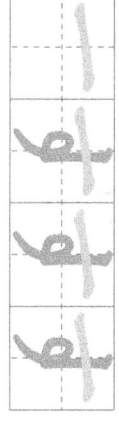
Pronounced like the 'su' in super.

chi

Pronounced just like the 'chi' in tai-chi.

na
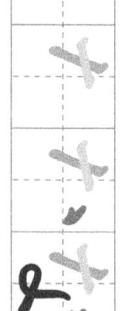
Pronounced like the 'na' in narwhal.

se

Pronounced like 'say' but with less 'y' sound.

tsu
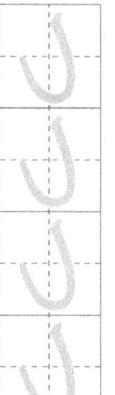
Pronounced just as the 'tsu' in tsunami, with a silent 't'.

ni
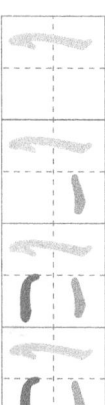
Pronounced like the 'nee' in needle but shorter.

so
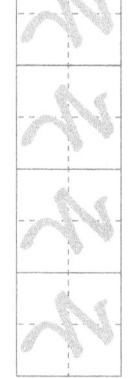
Pronounced like the 'so' in soy.

te
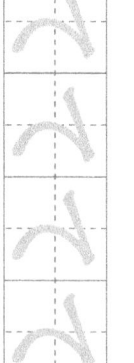
Pronounced just like the 'te' in ten.

nu
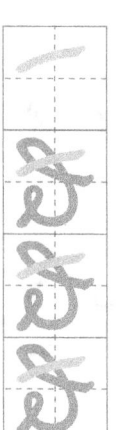
Pronounced like the 'noo' in noodles but short.

ta
Pronounced like the 'ta' in target.

to
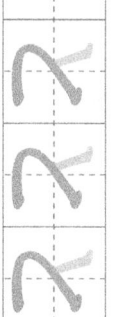
Pronounced like the 'to' in tick-tock.

ne
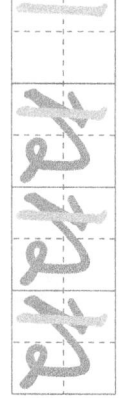
Pronounced like the 'ne' in nest.

no
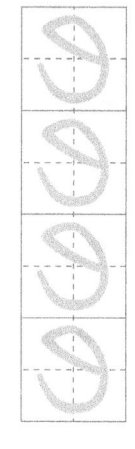
Pronounced like the 'no' in nose.

he
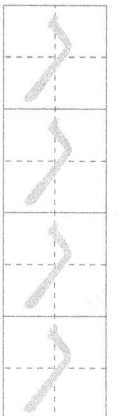
Pronounced like the 'he' in Helen.

mu
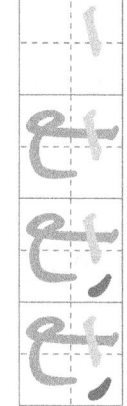
Pronounced like 'moo' but in move.

ha

Pronounced as the 'ha' when laughing, like ha-ha.

ho
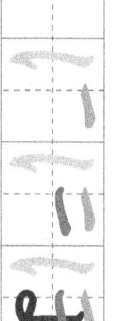
Pronounced like the 'ho' in home.

me
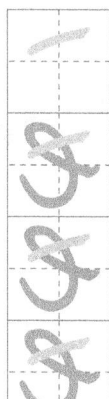
Pronounced like 'meh' like the 'me' in mend.

hi
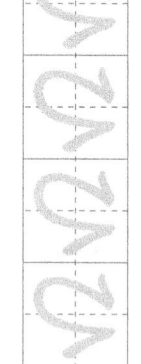
Pronounced like the 'he' in He or She.

ma
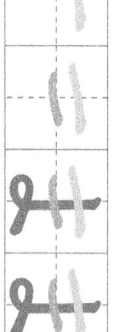
Pronounced like the 'ma' in market.

mo
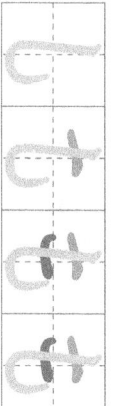
Pronounced just like the 'mo' in more.

fu

Pronounced as 'hu' like the word 'who'.

mi
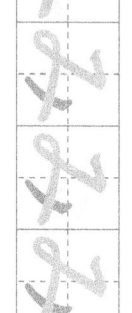
Pronounced just like 'me'.

ya
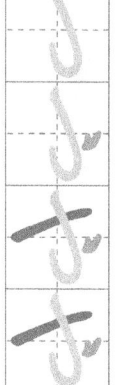
Pronounced like the 'ya' in yard.

り	れ	よ	ゆ
わ	ろ	る	ら
		ん	を

yu
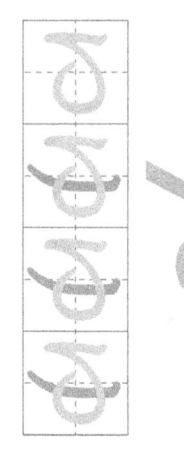
Pronounced like the 'u' in universal.

ra

Pronounced like the 'ra' in ramen.

wo
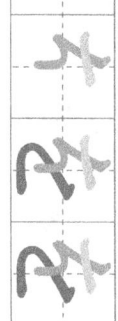 
Pronounced like the 'oh' in woah, with a silent 'w'.

yo
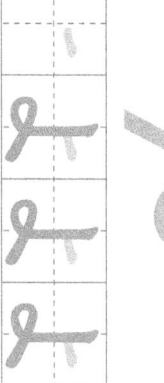
Pronounced just like the 'yo' in yo-yo.

ru
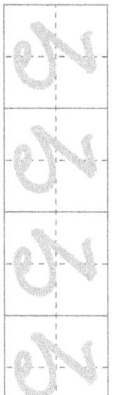 
Pronounced like the 'rew' in brew.

n*
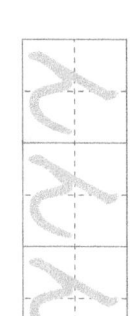
Pronounced like just the 'n' sound in ink.

re

Pronounced like the 're' in rent.

ro
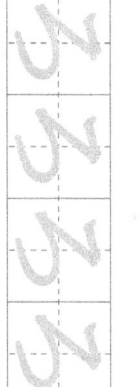 
Pronounced like the 'ro' in road.

ri

Pronounced like the 'ree' in reef.

wa
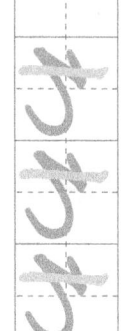 
Pronounced like the 'wa' in wagon.

a
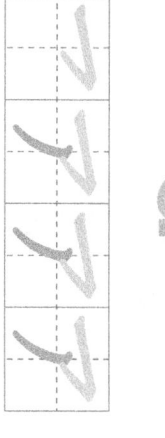
Pronounced like the 'a' in car or father, but shorter.

i
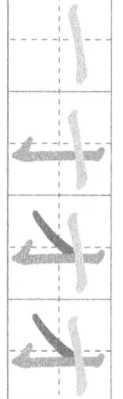
Pronounced like the 'ee' in eel.

u
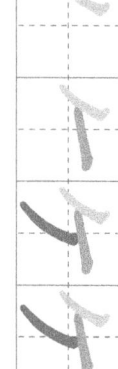
Pronounced like the 'oo' in zoo.

e
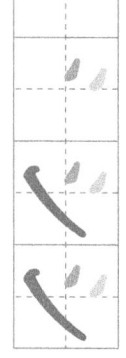
Pronounced as 'eh' like the 'e' in men.

o
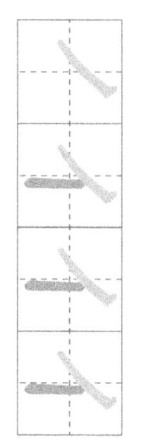
Pronounced like the 'o' in original.

ka
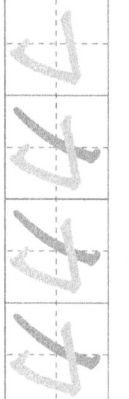
Pronounced like 'car' but without the 'r' sound.

ki

Pronounced like 'key'.

ku

Pronounced like the 'koo' in cuckoo.

ke
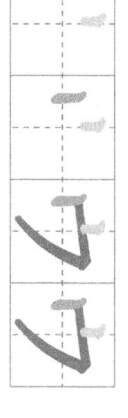
Pronounced like the 'ke' in Kenneth.

ko
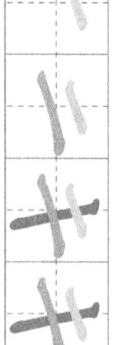
Pronounced like the 'co' in core.

sa
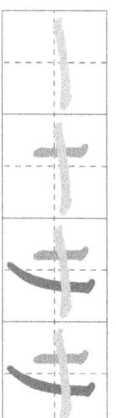
Pronounced like the 'sa' in sardines.

shi
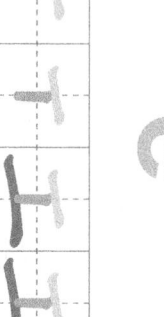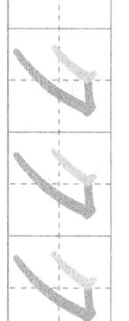
Pronounced 'shee' as in sheet.

又	艹	十
女	丷	刂
丿	彳	攵
丹	卜	木

su
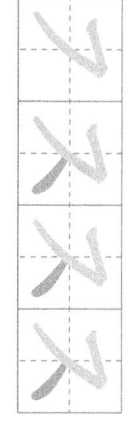
Pronounced like the 'su' in super.

chi
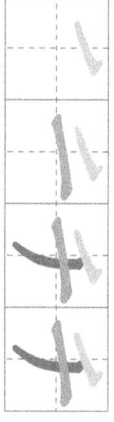
Pronounced just like the 'chi' in tai-chi.

na
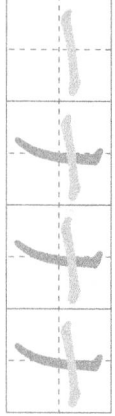
Pronounced like the 'na' in narwhal.

se
Pronounced like 'say' but with less 'y' sound.

tsu
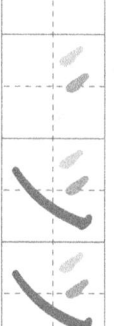
Pronounced just as the 'tsu' in tsunami, with a silent 't'.

ni
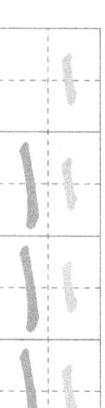
Pronounced like the 'nee' in needle but shorter.

so
Pronounced like the 'so' in soy.

te
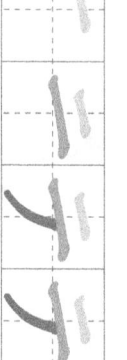
Pronounced just like the 'te' in ten.

nu

Pronounced like the 'noo' in noodles but short.

ta
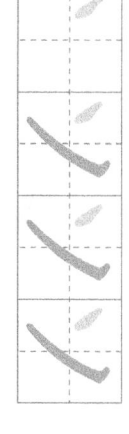
Pronounced like the 'ta' in target.

to
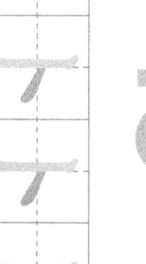
Pronounced like the 'to' in tick-tock.

ne
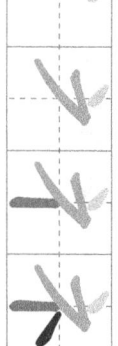
Pronounced like the 'ne' in nest.

no
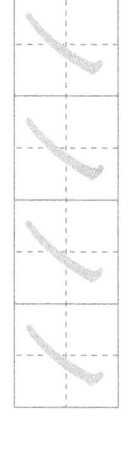
Pronounced like the 'no' in nose.

ha
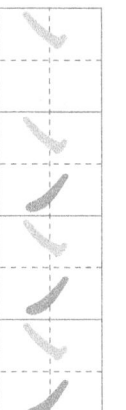
Pronounced as the 'ha' when laughing, like ha-ha.

hi
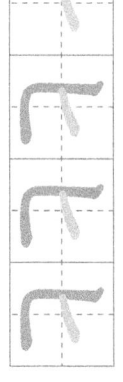
Pronounced like the 'he' in He or She.

fu
Pronounced as 'hu' like the word 'who'.

he
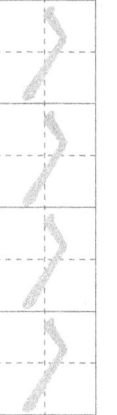
Pronounced like the 'he' in Helen.

ho
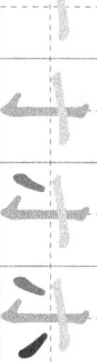
Pronounced like the 'ho' in home.

ma
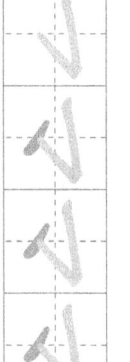
Pronounced like the 'ma' in market.

mi
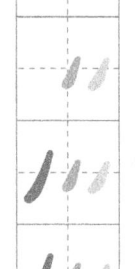
Pronounced just like 'me'.

mu
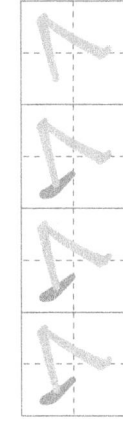
Pronounced like 'moo' but in move.

me
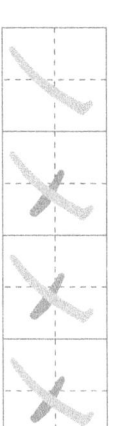
Pronounced like 'meh' like the 'me' in mend.

mo
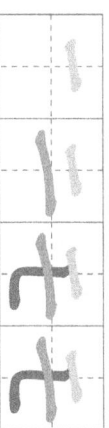
Pronounced just like the 'mo' in more.

ya
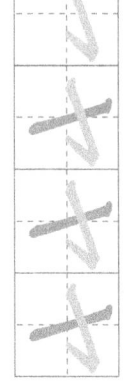
Pronounced like the 'ya' in yard.

yu
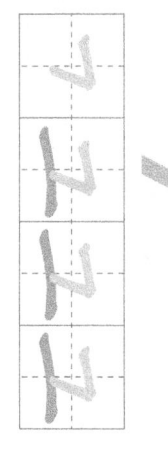
Pronounced like the 'u' in universal.

re
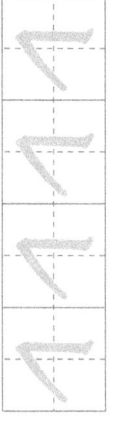
Pronounced like the 're' in rent.

wo
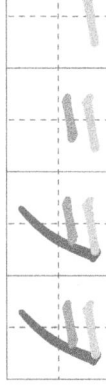
Pronounced like the 'oh' in woah, with a silent 'w'.

yo
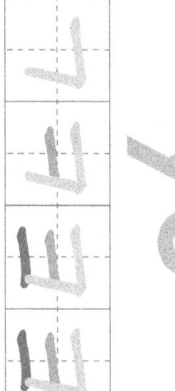
Pronounced just like the 'yo' in yo-yo.

ra
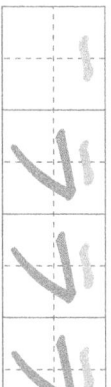
Pronounced like the 'ra' in ramen.

n*
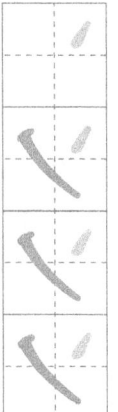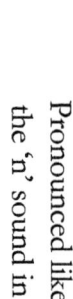
Pronounced like just the 'n' sound in ink.

ru
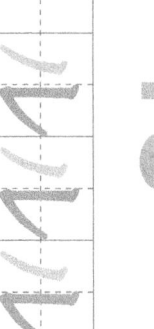
Pronounced like the 'rew' in brew.

ro
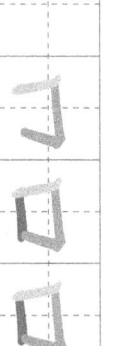
Pronounced like the 'ro' in road.

ri

Pronounced like the 'ree' in reef.

wa
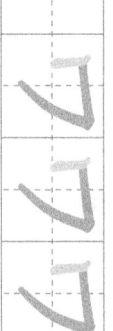
Pronounced like the 'wa' in wagon.

ありがとう
arigatou

Thank you!

Thank you for choosing our book!

You are now well on your way to learning how to read, write and speak Japanese, and we hope that you enjoyed our Hiragana & Katakana workbook.

If you enjoyed learning with us, we would very much like to hear about your progress in a review!

We are always eager to learn if there is anything we can do to make our books better for future students. We are committed to making the best language learning content available so please do get in touch with us via email if you had a problem with any of the content in this book:

hello@polyscholar.com

POLYSCHOLAR

www.polyscholar.com

© Copyright 2020 George Tanaka - All rights reserved.

Legal Notice: This book is copyright protected. This book is only for personal use. The content contained within this book may not be reproduced, duplicated or transmitted without direct written permission from the author or the publisher. You cannot amend, distribute, sell, use, quote or paraphrase any part of the content within this book, without the consent of the author or publisher.

www.ingramcontent.com/pod-product-compliance
Lightning Source LLC
Chambersburg PA
CBHW060506240426
43661CB00007B/936